Genealogical History

WITH

SHORT SKETCHES AND FAMILY RECORDS

OF THE

EARLY SETTLERS OF WEST SIMSBURY

NOW

CANTON, CONNECTICUT

BY

Abiel Brown, Esq.

HERITAGE BOOKS
2022

HERITAGE BOOKS

AN IMPRINT OF HERITAGE BOOKS, INC.

Books, CDs, and more—Worldwide

For our listing of thousands of titles see our website
at
www.HeritageBooks.com

A Facsimile Reprint
Published 2022 by
HERITAGE BOOKS, INC.
Publishing Division
5810 Ruatan Street
Berwyn Heights, MD 20740

Originally published
Hartford:
Press of Case, Tiffany and Company
1856
(Re-printed, N.Y., 1899)

Cover photograph: jessica45 from Pixabay.

— Publisher's Notice —
In reprints such as this, it is often not possible to remove blemishes from the original. We feel the contents of this book warrant its reissue despite these blemishes and hope you will agree and read it with pleasure.

International Standard Book Number
Paperbound: 978-1-55613-928-4

Notice Introductory and Commendatory.

ON the publication or proposed publication of a book, it is legitimate to inquire, What is the object? Why another book? Why this? And it is too late in the world's time to deny the right, or question the propriety of thus asking for the reason of things.

This little unpretending volume, made up in great part of names, which had a local habitation in a very rural district, may seem to many uncalled for, and not to justify the labor and expense of its compilation and printing. But if it has nothing to boast of renowned characters beyond what is common to other localities and settlements in its vicinity, it still contains the seeds of things whose productions it becomes us well to study and understand.

As to names, the world is full of them, because it is full of things, and we have the highest authority for their use and record. When in the beginning God made the light, he gave it a name; he called the light day, the darkness he called night; the firmament, heaven; the dry land, earth; and the gathering of the waters he called seas. So, when he made man he called him Adam, and the helpmate for him, Eve; and these two were the head and progenitors of all our race. This is ample authority for names and their record. We have also equal authority in the Scripture genealogy for the registration of families, as such, in their local habitation.

The sons of Noah, Shem, Ham and Japhet, went forth out of the Ark, and of them the whole earth was overspread. Again, it is written, (Gen. 10:32,) These are the families of the sons of Noah, after their generations in their nations, and by them were the nations divided in the earth after the flood.

Every settlement has a beginning, a development, a progress. Every smaller settlement is an integral part of the larger; the district of the town, the town of the county, the county of the state, the state of the nation; yea, the nations make but one world. Families make a settlement, and if the origin and progress of a settlement contain items of value and of interest, to no others, surely they must to themselves and to their descendants. This work was undertaken some two years since, by ABIEL BROWN, Esq., a descendent of one of the first settlers, in the west part of Simsbury, now Canton, not in anticipation of any personal pecuniary profit, but for the collection and preservation of facts and incidents connected with the first settlers of the town, which it was believed, might be useful to the present, and coming generations.

In the prosecution of his undertaking, he was stimulated by the urgent request of many of the younger men of the place who expressed their conviction that such a record, made and preserved, would be invaluable to the inhabitants of the town in after time. The result, extending far beyond the first intention of the author, is short sketches, with the record of about one hundred and eighty-five families, extending down to not far from the close of the ministry of Rev. Jeremiah Hallock.

The materials of the work have been gathered by an examination of monuments and burial records in the town of Canton, of monuments and probate records in the town of Simsbury; some items were collected from Windsor, and some from Plymouth, Mass. Beside these and similar sources of information, the author was largely indebted to the storehouse of his own memory, by the strength and tenacity of which, he, above all was the man fitted for such an undertaking. The man who could "remember where he was and what he did every day in a single year,"* was of all, the man to undertake such a labor.

* A remark he once made to his nephew, Heman Humphrey, D. D., Pittsfield, Massachusetts.

Perfection in this work is not claimed. The lapse of more than one hundred years and the extreme paucity of family records make this impossible. The amount of labor, both physical and mental the work has cost, can be understood by those only who have themselves been engaged in some work of this kind.

Mr. Brown expressed to his family, his felt obligation to many individuals who had rendered him essential aid in his undertaking, particularly to Ephraim Mills, Esq., of Canton, and John O. Pettibone, Esq., of Simsbury.

Expressing his deep regret that we know so little of our ancestors, and in the hope that his efforts might contribute to an increased acquaintanceship with the families, the character, and the influence of the past generations, he was suddenly called from all earthly cares and efforts, leaving the work he had in hand to be completed and disposed of by others.

The work is rather a record than a history; a record of families, and noteworthy events, which we doubt not will interest and instruct the people of Canton, and such, at least, in other parts of the land and world as look back to this town as the place of their nativity and of very many of their most hallowed memories. J. B.

CANTON, May, 1856.

GENEALOGICAL HISTORY.

Lieut. DAVID ADAMS. He removed from the old parish to West Simsbury about the year 1743. He resided in the second house north of the north burying ground, the west side of the highway. The house is now demolished

Parents.	Born.	Died.	Age.	
David Adams,	1716,	1801,	85.	
Mindwell Case,	1718,	1813,	95.	Daughter of Daniel Case.

Children.	Born.	Died.	Age.	
David,	1740,	1834,	94.	Married Hannah Edgerton.
Mary,	1742,	1791,	49.	Married Noah Case, 2d.
Abel,	1746,	1776,	30.	Married Anna Roberts.
Ezra,	1751,	1837,	86.	Married Hannah Wilcox.
George.				Married Sabra Miller.
Sarah,	1755,	1834,	79.	Married Darius Moses.
Lydia,	1757,	1793,	36.	Married Prince Taylor.
Mercy,	1760,	1787,	27.	Died single.
Chloe,	1761,	1828,	67.	Married Gad Bliss.

Two children died in infancy. Average age 64 years 7 months.

This family was composed of eleven children; nine lived to adult years, and two died in infancy.

DAVID ADAMS, Jr., son of Lieut. David Adams, was the owner and resided on the premises now owned by Oliver C. and Geo. W. Adams. He married Miss Hannah Edgerton; they left no children.

Parents.	Born.	Died.	Age.
David Adams,	1740,	1834,	94.
Hannah Edgerton,	1743,	1828,	85.

ABEL ADAMS. He was the second son of Lieut. David Adams; he resided on the farm now known by the name of the Minor place, being the east part of the farm of Israel W. Graham, Esq.

He married Anna daughter of William and Hannah Roberts. He, with two of his children, died in September, 1776, of the fatal epidemic which then prevailed in the army and in the country. His widow afterward married Daniel Graham.

Parents.	Born.	Died.	Age.
Abel Adams,	1746,	1776,	30.
Anna Roberts,	1748,	1821,	73.

Children.	Born.	Died.	Age.	
William,	1765.			Married Miss Hayes.
Martin,	1769.			Married Ruth Hart from R. I.
Samantha,	1774,	1776,	2.	
Roswell,	1776,	1776.		

EZRA ADAMS, Esq., was the third son of Lieut. David Adams. He married Hannah, daughter of Col. Amos Wilcox. He resided the fore part of his family state, west of the brook and meadow, on the premises now owned by Averett Wilcox, Esq. He afterward built the house now occupied by Averett Wilcox, Esq.

Parents.	Born.	Died.	Age.
Ezra Adams,	1751,	1837,	86.
Ist wife, Hannah Wilcox,	1755,	1801,	46.
2nd wife, Hannah Seymour,	1766,	1824,	58.

Children.	Born.	Died.	Age.	
Mindwell, (idiot,)	1773,	1777,	4.	
Ezra, Jun.	1775,	1836,	61.	Married Abigail Hurlbut.
Abel, (idiot,)	1777,	1786,	9.	
Hannah, (idiot,)	1780,	1791,	11.	
Tracy, (idiot,)	1788,	1800,	12.	
Laura,	1790,			Married Decius Humphrey.
Infant,	1793,	1793.		
David,	1798.			Died in Clarksville, Tennessee.

In this family of eight children but two were married; four of them although born with usual capacities, soon sunk into and died in a state of idiocy, which was a great trial to their parents.

HEZEKIAH ADAMS, son of Thomas Adams. He removed from the east part of Simsbury about the year 1749, and resided on the farm and site now owned and occupied by Albert F. Bidwell. His first wife was Lydia Phelps, by whom he had six children.

Parents.	Born.	Died.	Age.	
Hezekiah Adams,	1727,	1784,	57.	
1st wife, Lydia Phelps,	1725,	1760,	35.	Daughter of Abraham Phelps.
2nd wife, Sarah Phelps,	1738.			Daughter of Thomas Phelps.

Children by his 1st wife.	Born.	Died.	Age.	
Lydia,	1751,	1773,	21.	
Dorcas,	1753,	1794,	41.	Married Aaron Richards.
Lucina.				Married Jesse Steele.

3 children died in infancy.

Children by his 2nd wife.	Born.	Died.	Age.	
Hezekiah,	1763,	1793,	29.	An idiot.
Sarah,	1767,	1776,	9.	
Roger,	1770,	1838,	68.	Married Ruth Hays.
Charles,	1772,	1801,	29.	Married Chloe Johnson.

Sarah,	1776, 1800, 24.	Died single.
Amos,	1783, 1784.	

Of this family seven lived to adult years; four died in infancy, and one aged nine years.

Roger, who was a clergyman, was a man of more than common ability; he had two sons, twin brothers, born 1796, who entered the ministry; their names were Erastus Homer, minister of ——————, and James Watson, D. D., minister of Syracuse.

NATHANIEL ALFORD. He removed from the old parish to West Simsbury about the year 1739. He resided on what is now called the missionary lot on the east hill.

Parents.	Born. Died. Age.
Nathaniel Alford,	1698.
Experience Holcomb.	1707.

Children.	Born. Died. Age.	
Hannah,	1727, 1811, 84.	Married Isaac Messenger.
Isabel,	1733, 1818, 85.	Married John Hill.
Susan,	1735,	Married Joseph Tiff.
Nathaniel, Jun.,	1737, 1818, 81.	Married Abigail Hill.
	1739.	Smith, known as Noggy Smith.
Lugia,	1799.	Married Soloman Thomas.
Rhoda,		Married Philip Jarvis.

One daughter married a Bettes and afterward a Heacox, but the particulars are not known. All the children married and had children.

NATHANIEL ALFORD, Jun., or 2d, was a son of Nathaniel Alford, Sen. He married Abigail, daughter of John Hill, Sen., in 1760. He resided on the premises now owned by Luther Higley, Esq., and now occupied by Norton Case.

Parents.	Born.	Died.	Age.
Nathan Alford,	1737,	1818,	81.
Abigail Hill,	1737,	1818,	81.

Children.	Born.	Died.	Age.	
Eber,	1760,	1844,	84.	Married, 1st, Esther Humphrey; 2d, Faithe Spencer.
Nathaniel Jun. or 3d,	1763,	1823,	60.	
Marbill,				Died single.
Charlotte,	1776,	1850,	74.	Married 1st, Abraham Moses, Jun.; 2d, Rufus Garret; 3d, Amasa Mills.
Arba,				Eunice Case.
Lora.				Removed to state of Maine.
Eliphalet,	1777.			Married a daughter of Joseph Segur.
Marbill.				

JOSEPH BACON, son of Maskel Bacon, Sen., with his wife, settled in family state about the year 1772. He resided on land which now forms the north part of the farm of Loin H. Humphrey; it is now known by the name of the Bacon place. In 1806 he removed to the region of Onondaga, State of New York.

Parents.	Born.	Died.	Age.
Joseph Bacon,	1751,	1833,	82.
Mary Edgerton,	1753,	1849,	86.

Children.	Born.	Died.	Age.	
Infant,		1773.		
Infant,		1775.		
Joseph, Jun.,	1776.			Married Penlope Garrett.
Anna,	1778.			Married Azariah Barber.
A son,	1780.			Died.
Diadama,	1782.			Married Benoni Jones.
John,	1785.			Married Sarah Kenyon.
Mary,	1787.			Married Samuel Goddard.
Phineas,	1783.			Married Phily Norton.

One child died in 1780. One child died in 1793.

JAMES BEACH was a resident of Canton. He commenced family state about 1776. He was by trade a blacksmith. He lived on the farm now owned by Asa Brown. He removed to Sandisfield about 1795. He had two sons; the oldest born as early as 1776; nothing further is known respecting this family.

OLIVER BRONSON, a native of Guilford, Conn., was employed by the people of Simsbury, about 1773, to teach vocal music, in the society. This occurrence led to his acquaintance with Miss Sarah Merrell, daughter of William Merrell, Sen., which finally resulted in their being united in marriage. He then became a resident of West Simsbury, and with his partner and family resided on land now owned by Harvey Mills. The house was situated between the house of Harvey Mills, and Ozias Pike. All their children, save the youngest, were born in this town. He became quite celebrated as a teacher of vocal music, and was employed in several of the most popular churches in Connecticut, in addition to his own adopted society. He removed to Old Simsbury in 1786, and there resided till about 1802; then removed to Cazenova, New York.

Parents.	Born. Died. Age.	
Oliver Bronson.		
Sarah Merrell,	1752.	

Children.	Born. Died. Age.	
Willys,	1774.	
Simeon,	1776.	Married Cyntha Gleason.
Oliver,	1779.	
Manna,	1782.	
Sarah,	1785.	Married Taylor, father of Green Taylor.
Green, C.		Born in Simsbury; became chief judge of the supreme court of the State of New York; also attorney general.

THOMAS BIDWELL, SEN. He with his wife, whose name was Ruhamah Pinney, came from Windsor about the year 1740. He settled on the premises that fell to his son Thomas, and said premises have remained in the possession of the Bidwell family to the present time.

Parents.	Born.	Died.	Age.	
Thomas Bidwell, Sen.,	1701,	1746,	45.	Was buried in New Hartford, on Town Hill.
Ruhamah Pinney,		1776.		The widow married Ephraim Wilcox.

Children.	Born.	Died.	Age.	
Abigail,	1734,	1810,	76.	Married Thomas Cone.
Ruhamah,		1814,	71.	Married James Cornish.
Thomas, Jun.,	1738,	1802,	64.	Married Esther Orton; she died 1823, aged 87.
Prudence.				Married Aaron Pinney.

EPHRAIM WILCOX. After the death of Thomas Bidwell, Sen., Ephraim Wilcox, married his widow; they had five children.

Children.	Born.	Died.	Age.	
Philander.				
Martin.				
Asa.				
Jehiel.				
Chloe.				Married Elijah Humphrey.

DEAC. THOMAS BIDWELL. He with his wife settled in the east part of New Hartford, (now Canton,) on land left him by his father.

Parents.	Born.	Died.	Age.
Thomas Bidwell,	1738,	1802,	64.
Esther Orton,	1737,	1823,	87.

Children.	Born. Died. Age.	
Jehiel,	1660, 1777, 16.	Was taken prisoner at Fort Washington, November 1776, and died from harsh treatment, Jan., 1777.
Riverius,	1762, 1822, 59.	Married Phebe Roberts; died 1837, aged 76.
Thomas, Jun.,	1764, 1848, 83.	Married Lavinia Humphrey.
Norman,	1768, 1849, 78.	Married Falla Hills.
Lois,	1773, 1828, 55.	Married Dr. Abiram Peet.
Jasper,	1775, 1848, 73.	Married Lucy Richards.

A GENEALOGICAL SKETCH OR HISTORY OF THE ANCESTRY OF THE BROWN FAMILY.

PETER BROWN, one of that memorable little band who landed at Plymouth, Mass., Dec. 22d, 1620, appears by traditional accounts, in connection with many historical facts and other sketches of record, with other corroborating circumstances, to be the progenitor of the Windsor Browns. He came to America single; was by trade a carpenter; he died 1633. Peter Brown, 2d, was born 1632; he married Mary Gillett, 1658; his monument in Windsor burying-ground tells us that he died Oct., 1692, aged 60 years. He had four sons, Peter, John, Jonathan, and Cornelius. They all had numerous families. In 1694 they exchanged lands that were their fathers with the selectmen of the town of Windsor. John, 1st, the 2d son, was married to Miss Elizabeth Loomis, 1692; she died 1723. They had three sons and eight daughters. The names of the sons were John, 2d, Isaac, and Daniel. John, 2d, the eldest son and the fifth of the family was born March, 1700; married Miss Mary Eggleston, March, 1725. He died 1790, aged 90 years. His wife died 1789, aged 87. They had two sons and seven daughters. Mary, the oldest of the family, remained single through life and died aged 100 years.

Margery married David Filley; she died 1775, aged about 45; she left no children alive. The other daughters all died in childhood and youth, most of them with the canker rash; their deaths were in quick succession. The names of the two sons were John, 3d, and Ezra. John, 3d, the oldest of them, was born November 4th, 1728; married Miss Hannah Owen, 1758. She was the daughter of Elijah and Hannah Owen. Her grandfather, Isaac Owen, was one of the first settlers in Turkey Hills; her mother was daughter of Brewster Higley. Elijah Owen died September, 1741, aged 35; his relict died 1806, aged 90. After the death of Mr. Owen, she married Pelatiah Mills, and was the mother of a numerous Mills family. The names of the Owen children were Rebecca, Elijah and Hannah; names of the Mills children were Pelatiah, Samuel, Roger, Patty, Eli, Frederick, Susannah and Elihu. John Brown, 3d, was chosen Captain of the train-band, in West Simsbury in the spring of 1776. His commission from Governor Trumbull, bears date May 23d, 1776. A regimental order from Col. Jonathan Pettibone to Capt. John Brown, bears date June 11th, 1776, and reads as follows:

To John Brown, Captain of the 8th Company in the 18 *Regiment of the Militia in the Colony of Connecticut.*

WHEREAS the General Assembly have Enacted, that One third Part of the 2d, 3d, 4th, 7th, 8th, 9th, and 20th Regiments, and One quarter part of the other Regiments of the Militia, or a Number equivalent thereto, be forthwith inlisted or detached, from the Limits of the several Regiments in this Colony, to be held in Readiness, for the Defence of this or any of the adjoining Colonies; and the Colonels or chief Officers of the respective Regiments, are to issue the necessary Orders therefor.

These are therefore to command you, forthwith to convene your Company, and also give Notice to, and request the Attendance, at the same Time and Place of all others, within the Limits thereof, who are obliged to keep Arms, and are between Sixteen and Fifty-Five Years of Age, and being so convened, to inlist out of any of them (or otherwise as soon as may be) the Number aforesaid, and if a sufficient number shall not voluntarily inlist, you are hereby farther commanded, with the Advice and Assistance of the other Commission Officers, to detatch and impress, out of your said Company, such Number of able bodied Men, as shall appear to be wanting, of the enlisted Men, to make up the Complement aforesaid; and make Return of your Doings in the Premises, to me within Six days after said Men shall be inlisted, or detached, taking Care to return the Names of the Men enlisted, and the Names of those detached, distinguishing between those of the Militia and those who are not.

Given under my Hand, in Simsbury the 11th Day of June, Anno Domini, 1776.

JON. PETTIBONE, Colonel.

Form of Inlistment, viz.,

We the Subscribers, of Simsbury, in the County of Hartford, each for himself do hereby acknowledge to have voluntarily inlisted to serve as Minute-Men for the Defence of this and adjoining Colonies, and engage to hold ourselves in constant readiness, agreeable to the Tenor and Regulations of an Act passed by the General Assembly of this Colony in May, 1776, entitled "An Act for Raising and Equipping a Body of Minute-Men, to be held in Readiness for the better Defence of this Colony;" and under the Command of such Officers as shall be appointed agreeable to the Direction of said Act. As Witness our Hands.

The company was soon raised and with it, Captain Brown marched and joined the army at New York, where, after about two months service he was taken sick with the dysentary and died September 3d, 1776, leaving a wife and eleven children, the eldest being but eighteen years of age, and the oldest son but nine.

CAPT. JOHN BROWN. He came from Wintonbury, (now Bloomfield,) with his wife who was Hannah Owen, a descendant from the first John Owen, of Windsor. He settled in West Simsbury in the year 1755, on the premises now occupied by his son, Abiel Brown, in the Center school district.

Parents.	Born. Died. Age.	
John Brown,	1728, 1776, 48.	Died in the army at N. York.
Hannah Owen,	1740, 1831, 91.	

Children.	Born. Died. Age.	
Hannah,	1758, 1825, 66.	2d wife of Solomon Humphrey.
Azubah,	1760, 1812, 52.	Married Michael Barber.
Esther,	1762, 1838, 76.	Married Timothy Case.
Margery,	1764, 1820, 56,	2d wife of David Giddings. 2d wife of Prince Taylor.
Lucinda,	1765, 1814, 49.	2d wife of Russel Borden.
John, 4th,	1767, 1849, 82.	1st wife, Millisent Gaylord; 2d, widow Abi Case.
Frederick,	1769, 1848, 78.	1st wife, Catharine Case; 2d, Chloe S. Pettibone.
Owen,	1771, 1856, 85.	1st wife Ruth Mills; 2d Sarah Root; 3d, Abi Hinsdale.
Thede,	1773, 1846, 74.	2d wife of William Merrells.
Roxy, R.,	1775, 1855, 80.	Married Alexander Humphrey.
Abiel,	1776, 1856, 79.	Born farther west; married Anna Lord, of Lyme.

The average age of this family of children, is about seventy years, and six months.

ABIEL BROWN, ESQ., the compiler of this work, died of typhus fever, March 15th, 1856, aged 79 years, 4 months. He lived and died in the same house where he was born.

Parents.	Born. Died. Age.	
Abiel Brown,	1776, 1856, 79.	
Anna Lord,	1788,	Still living, 1856.

Children.	Born. Died. Age.	
William Ely,	1807.	Married Nancy Barber.
An infant,	1810, 1810	
John, 5th,	1811.	Married 1st, Fanny Case; 2d, Laura Case.
Selden Holmes,	1813.	Married Phebe Hodge.
Elizur Owen,	1816.	Married 1st, Mariah Clinton; 2d, Mary Ann Loomis.
Eliza Ann,	1822, 1845, 23.	

Dr. SAMUEL BARBER, the subject of these historical sketches, had the reputation of a good citizen, although somewhat eccentric in his habits and not unfrequently impulsive in his actions. He doted much in his skill in roots and herbs; was famous as a hunter, the woods at that time affording an abundance of game. In one of his hunting excursions in Norfolk, accompanied by some of his sons they chased a large panther into his den, and how to dislodge him from his hiding place was the first question to be solved. The old gentleman, nothing daunted, Putnam like, descended into the cavern; after grouping his way some distance the panther not relishing this intrusion upon his retreat suddenly turned and made for the entrance of his den which he accomplished by closely squeezing by his bold intruder. The panther, on his arrival at the mouth of the den, seeing the party without prepared to give him battle, stood motionless, when one of the sons discharged a ball through his body and intestines which produced no emotion, the animal sullenly retaining his position. This act of the son called forth a sharp reprimand from his father, for his not taking a more effective aim, and calling for his gun the old gentleman discharged a ball through the head of the animal which put an end to his existence. This exploit may justly be put on a parallel with the famous story of "Putnam and the Wolf."

The family of Barbers were among the earliest and most conspicuous of West Simsbury and a more extended notice of them is here given. The immediate ancestor of the family of Barbers who settled in West Simsbury was Samuel Barber who died about 1725. He was a descendant of the first Thomas Barber, of Windsor. He married Mercy Holcomb, granddaughter of the first Thomas Holcomb. This Mercy died 1787, aged 96. She removed from the old parish to West Simsbury in the year 1738, with her four sons, Samuel, Thomas, Jonathan and John, and her daughters, Mercy, wife of Ephraim Buel, and Sarah, wife of John Case, 4th. Her sons settled on Cherries Brook, on lands contiguous to each other, comprising the meadows and best lands in the center school district in Canton. The family were noted for their habits of immigration and are to be found in various states of the Union; few of the descendants (although numerous) are to be met with in the town of Canton.

DR. SAMUEL BARBER. He settled on the farm now owned by Norton Case. He married for his first wife Tryphene Humphrey, daughter of Samuel Humphrey, by whom he had seven sons. Her monument is the oldest in the town of Canton. His second wife was Hannah, daughter of Capt. Noah Humphrey, who commanded a company at the capture of Havanna, in 1762. By this marriage he had seven children, four sons and three daughters.

Parents.	Born. Died. Age.	
Samuel Barber,	1714, 1797, 83.	
1st wife, Tryphene Humphrey,	1722, 1752, 30.	Daughter of Samuel Humphrey; the first person interred in the south burying ground. Her monument is the oldest in town, bearing date, 1752.
2d wife, Hannah Humphrey.	1726, 1819, 93.	Daughter of Capt. Noah Humphrey, who commanded a company that went to Havanna in 1762.

Children by 1st wife.	Born. Died. Age.	
Samuel,	1740, 1780, 40.	Married —— Cowles.
Timothy,	1742, 1817, 75.	Married Keturah Riley.
Joseph,	1744, 1807, 63.	Married Leah Grover.
David,	1746.	Married Deborah Adams.
Elijah,	1748, 1820, 72.	Married Sarah Pettibone.
Ezekiel,	1750, 1806, 56.	Married Elizabeth Goddard.
Daniel,	1752, 1776, 24.	Died single in the army.

Children by 2d wife.	Born, Died, Age.	
Tryphene,	1755.	Married Nathaniel Johnson.
Joel,	1757.	Married Mary Phelps.
Hannah,	1759.	Married Aaron Rawls.
Sarah,	1761, 1829, 68.	Married John George Bandell.
Asahel,	1763, 1851, 88.	Married Mary Collar.
Jesse,	1766, 1813, 47.	Married Hepzibah Humphrey.
Giles,	1769, 1826, 57.	Married Mary Garret; still living, 1856.

The 2d wife Hannah, died in Canton at the house of her son Giles Barber.

This family of children, all lived to adult years and all had children excepting Timothy and Daniel.

ELIJAH BARBER, fifth son of Samuel and Tryphene Barber, married Sarah, daughter of Abel Pettibone about 1774. He resided on the premises now owned by his son Daniel Barber, near the center school-house.

Parents.	Born. Died. Age.
Elijah Barber,	1748, 1820, 73.
Sarah Pettibone,	1755, 1842, 88.

Children.	Born. Died. Age.	
Sarah,	1774, 1777, 3.	
Sarah,	1777.	Married William Barber.
Annis,	1780.	Married Ruluff Barber.
Lodama,	1782, 1796, 14.	Died single.

Elijah,	1785, 1786.	
Elijah, Jun.,	1787, 1804, 17.	
Daniel,	1789.	Married Anna Betts.
An infant,	1792, 1792.	
Joseph,	1794, 1804, 10.	

JOEL BARBER, first son of Samuel and Hannah Barber, married Mary Phelps. He erected a house at the foot of the west mountain, on land now belonging to Wm. H. Hallock, Esq. He resided there, until the death of his wife in 1784, when his family were partially separated for years. About the year 1792, he removed to the north-western part of Vermont.

It is understood that some time previous to 1812, he removed into Canada. The time of his death is not definitely known. The family all left Connectict in the year 1794, and it is not known who any of them connected in marriage with.

Parents.	Born. Died. Age.	
Joel Barber,	1757.	
Mary Phelps,	1755, 1784.	Daughter of Thomas Phelps, Sen.

Children.	Born. Died. Age.	
Joel, 2d.,	1776.	Was a self made, useful and highly-honored citizen, a judge of the court, and sustaining other important and responsible public stations.
Allen,	1778.	Was a respectable physician; was, with others, drowned while attempting to cross the river St. Lawrence at or near Montreal, 1806.
Lois,	1780.	
Clementia,	1783.	Was brought up in the family of Dea. Andrew Mills.

SERG THOMAS BARBER. He with his widowed mother, Mercy Barber, and his brothers Samuel, Jonathan and John, removed from the old parish to West Simsbury about the year 1738. He resided on the place lately owned by Hosea Case, deceased, and now owned by Warren C. Humphrey. He had ten children, five sons and five daughters, who all lived to marry and have children, except Elizabeth.

Parents.	Born. Died. Age.	
Thomas Barber,	1716, 1792, 76.	
Elizabeth Adams.	1716, 1899, 94.	Daughter of Samuel Adams.

Children.	Born. Died. Age.	
Jacob,	1738, 1817, 79.	Married Patience Lawrence.
Elizabeth,	1740, 1825, 85.	Married Samuel Leet.
Lucy,	1742, 1834, 92.	Married Moses Gains.
Abraham,	1744, 1835, 91.	Married Sarah Wood.
Mercy,	1747, 1787, 40.	Married Ebenezer Cowles.
Azariah,	1750, 1817, 67.	Married Elizabeth Humphrey.
Tryphene,	1752, 1824, 72.	Married 1st, Meekham McFarland; 2d, Castle.
Michael,	1754, 1836, 82.	Married Azubah Brown.
Job,	1756, 1848, 92.	Married Lola Mills.
Abigail,	1758, 1813, 55.	Married Peletiah Richards.

This family lived to a great age, the average at the time of their deaths being seventy-six years eight months.

Mr. Thomas Barber, was eminently known as a peacemaker in community, a constant attendant on public worship, and in early life was much attached to hunting and trapping.

JACOB BARBER, with his wife, settled in family state about the year 1764. He was the first son of Serg. Thomas Barber, and his wife daughter of Samuel Lawrence.

He resided on the north part of the farm now owned and occupied by Franklin Case; his house was on the west side of the highway, opposite the house of James Humphrey.

In the year 1788 he removed to Barkhamsted, in the neighhood called Ratlum; from this place he removed to the region of Cazanova, State of New York, in 1815.

Parents.	Born. Died. Age.
Jacob Barber	1738, 1817, 79.
Patience Lawrence,	1746, 1809, 63.

Children.	Born. Died. Age.	
Zimri,	1764.	Married Thanks Wilcox.
James,	1767.	Married Levina Humphrey.
Patience Satitha,	1769.	Married Roger Moses.
Ezekiel,	1772, 1772.	
Thomas,	1773.	Married Percy Merrell.
Peter,	1774.	Married Hannah Taylor.
Susannah,	1777.	Married Benjamin Hosford.
Candace,	1779.	Married Naaman Phelps.
Dan,	1782.	Married Sally Bishop.
Deliverance,	1784.	Married Darius Case.
Mercy,	1787.	Married ——— Johnson.
An infant,	1790.	

ABRAHAM BARBER, the second son of Serg. Thomas Barber, married about 1764. He was for a number of years a resident on the farm afterward owned by Michael Barber, and now owned by Martin Barber, son of Michael Barber. He about 1779, removed to the place lately owned by William and his son Chester Barber. From the latter place he, in the year 1786, removed into the town of Barkhamsted; from there he in the year 1794, removed out of the state.

Parents.	Born. Died. Age.
Abraham Barber,	1744, 1836, 92.
Sarah Wood.	

Children.	Born. Died. Age.	
Abraham, Jun.,	1767.	Married Hannah Higley.
Luman,	1770, 1796, 26.	Married Mehitable Lilley.
Job,	1775.	
Joseph,	1777.	
Two daughters.		Births not known.

MICHAEL BARBER, 4th son of Serg. Thomas Barber, married Azubah Brown. He resided on the farm previously owned by his brother Abraham.

Parents.	Born. Died. Age.	
Michael Barber,	1754, 1836, 82.	
Azubah Brown,	1760, 1812, 52.	

Children.	Born. Died. Age.	
Sophia,	1779.	
Michael, Jun.,	1780, 1810, 30.	Married Anna Taylor, she died 1820.
Levi,	1782, 1852, 70.	Married Ruth Taylor; she died 1849.
Azubah,	1785.	2d wife of Stephen H. Atwater
Lyman,	1790.	Married Huldah Sanford.
Martin,	1794.	Married Anna Church; died 1855.
Salmon,	1800.	Married 1st, Betsy Wilcox; 2d, Ann Richardson.

AZARIAH BARBER, third son of Serg. Thomas Barber. He commenced family state in 1798, on the farm left by his father. He afterward removed on to the farm now owned by Alvin Bacon.

Parents.	Born. Died. Age.	
Azariah Barber,	1750, 1817, 67.	
Elizabeth Humphrey,	1753, 1826, 73.	Daughter of Noah Humphrey, 2d.

Children.	Born. Died. Age.	
Azariah, Jun.,	1776, 1855, 79.	Married Anna Bacon.
William,	1778.	Married Sarah Barber.
An infant,	1781.	Died.
Elizabeth,	1782, 1796, 14.	
Elam,	1785.	
Charlotte,	1788, 1845, 57.	Married Treat Lambert.
Noah,	1791, 1854, 63.	Married Eliza Drake.
Almira,	1793.	Married Aza Moses.

JONATHAN BARBER. He with his wife came from the old parish of West Simsbury with his brothers Samuel, Thomas and John. He settled and built on the place a few rods south of the dwelling-house of the late Jesse L. Barber deceased. He lost his life at the seige and capture of Louisburg, in 1745.

Parents.	Born.	Died.	Age
Johnathan Barber,	1717,	1745,	28.
Jemima Cornish,		1791.	

Children.	Born.	Died.	Age.	
Jonathan,	1743,	1762,	19.	Died in the expedition against Havana; single.
Jemima,	1741.			Married Joseph Messenger.
Mary,	1742.			
Bildad,	1745,	1816,	71.	Born fatherless; married Lois Humphrey, and removed to the State of New York.

His descendants have become extinct in the town of Canton. His widow after his death married Jacob Pettibone. The Pettibone children were Jacob, David, Martha, and Susannah, wife of Isaac Ensign.

BILDAD BARBER, son of Jonathan and Jemima Barber, married Lois, daughter of Oliver Humphrey, Esq. He commenced his family state about 1768, on the farm left by his father, Jonathan Barber. The premises are now owned by Franklin Case, the heirs of Jesse L. Barber, and the heirs of the late Gardner Mills. His first dwelling-house stood a few rods south of the dwelling of widow Phebe Barber. He with most of his family removed to the region of Onondaga, State of New York. A. D., 1804, where he and his, spent the remainder of their days.

Parents.	Born.	Died.	Age.
Bildad Barber,	1745,	1816,	71.
Lois Humphrey,	1746,	1810,	64.

Children.	Born. Died. Age.	
Trueman,	1769.	Married Alice Beebe, of Naugatuck.
Johnathan,	1772.	Married Amelia Humphrey.
Humphrey,	1773, 1832, 59.	Married Azubah Willey.
Percy,	1777.	Married —— Norton.
Erastus,	1779.	Married Annah Steele.
Ruluff,	1782.	Married Annis Barber.
Lois,	1784.	
Two twins,	1788.	Both died.
Philo,	1793.	
Bildad,	1791.	

Humphrey, the third son, was a large man, standing six feet seven inches high. The family are now extinct in Canton.

JOHN BARBER. SEN., a younger brother of Samuel, Thomas and Jonathan, came from the old parish about the year 1740. He settled on the land now owned by Lucius Foot and others. He built the house that is now standing, 1856. He had five sons and three daughters; six of them grew up and settled in family state and left children.

Parents.	Born. Died. Age.
John Barber,	1719, 1799, 80.
Lydia Reed,	1725, 1806, 81.

Children.	Born. Died. Age.	
Lydia,	1747, 1783, 36.	Married Samuel Olcott.
John, Jun.,	1749, 1825, 76.	Married Betsey Case.
Reuben,	1751, 1825, 74.	Married Elizabeth Case.
Sarah,	1754, 1761, 7.	
Rhoda,	1756, 1761, 5.	Died by the kick of a horse.
Benjamin,	1759, 1835, 75.	Married Lydia Case.
Jonathan,	1763, 1817, 54.	Married Abi Merrell.
Abel,	1765, 1817, 52.	Married Chloe Case.

The above Reuben was the first person interred in the Center burying-ground.

JONATHAN BARBER, son of John Barber, Sen., with his wife Abi, daughter of Jonathan Merrell, 2d, lived and died on the place left by his father, situated in the Center school district.

Parents.	Born. Died. Age.	
Jonathan Barber,	1763, 1817, 54.	Married, 1786.
Abi Merrell,	1769, 1848, 79.	

Children.	Born. Died. Age.	
Seth,	1788.	1st wife, Thirza Hayden; 2d, Mehitable Cressy; 3d, Olive Cressy.
Clarinda,	1789.	Married Miles Foot.
Abi,	1791, 1796, 5.	
Henry,	1793.	Married Naomi Humphrey.
Abiah,	1794, 1808, 14.	
Pluma,	1796, 1815, 19.	
Linda,	1799.	Married Uriah Hosford.
Thirza,	1801.	Married Isaac Barnes.
Susannah,	1803.	Married Imri L. Spencer.
Eliza,	1806.	Married Henry A. Adams.
Nancy,	1808.	Married Wm. E. Brown.
Jonathan Sherman,	1812, 1847, 35.	Married Statira Church.
Harvey,	1814.	Married Lorinda Case.

JOHN BARBER, Jun., son of John Barber, Sen., married Elizabeth, daughter of Capt. Josiah Case, A. D., 1773. He resided on the farm previously owned by Moses Gaines, and now owned by Henry Barber.

Parents.	Born. Died. Age.	
John Barber,	1749, 1825, 76.	Married, A. D. 1773.
Elizabeth Case,	1752, 1817, 65.	

Children.	Born. Died. Age.	
An infant,	1774, 1774.	
Elizabeth, or Betsey,	1775, 1817, 42.	Roswell Barber's 1st wife.
Rhoda,	1777.	Married Gurdon Hurlbut.

Cyntha,	1779, 1840, 61.	Married Chauncy Sadd.
John, Jun.,	1782.	Married 1st, Delight G. Case; 2d, Fanny Hunt.
Abi,	1784.	Married 1st, Elisha Case, Jun., 2d, Dea. John Brown.
Sylvia,	1785, 1786.	
Sylvia,	1787.	Married Dan Case, Jun.
Luke,	1789.	Married 1st, Clara Foote; 2d, Lavinia Hosmer.
Austin,	1792.	Married Lucy Allen.

REUBEN BARBER, son of John Barber, Sen., married Elizabeth, daughter of Dea. Hosea Case, A. D. 1775. He first resided on lands now owned by Loin H. Humphrey, until 18—, afterwards on the premises now owned by his son, Alson Barber. He was the first person interred in the Center burying-ground.

Parents.	Born. Died. Age,	
Reuben Barber,	1751, 1825, 74.	Married A. D. 1775.
Elizabeth Case,	1753, 1839, 86.	

Children.	Born. Died, Age.	
Reuben, Jun.,	1776, 1841, 65.	Married Lucretia Sloan.
Mary,	1778, 1804, 26.	Married Jonathan Noble.
Sadosa,	1780,	Married Sarah Cleaveland.
Elizabeth,	1782.	Married 1st, Josiah Harrison; 2d, Zimri Barber, Jun.
Phebe,	1785, 1838, 53.	Married Uri Cooke.
Hosea,	1788.	Married Hannah Fuller.
Starling,	1790, 1801, 11.	Died of a fractured head.
Alson,	1792.	Married Hannah Humphrey.
Sarah,	1794, 1822, 28.	Married Harvey Pike.

DANIEL BARBER, son of Serg. Thomas Barber, resided for a while in West Simsbury. The time of his settlement is not known. He resided on the place now occupied by Amos L. Spencer. He was living in this town in 1767; he had lost nearly all of his property, and the place was soon occupied by Caleb Spencer.

Parents.	Born. Died. Age.
Daniel Barber,	1732, 1779, 47.
Martha Phelps,	1739, 1822, 85.

Children.	Born. Died. Age.	
Daniel,	1756.	Married Chloe, widow of John Case.
Rosetta,	1758.	Married Jacob Pettibone, Jun.
Martha,	1760.	Married Asahel Holcomb, Jun.
Jared,	1764.	
Israel,	1765.	
Russel,	1767.	
Roswell,	1770.	Married Betsey Barber.
Calvin,	1772, 1846, 74.	Married Roena Humphrey, daughter of Maj. Elihu Humphrey.
Sarah,	1775.	Married George Fisher.
Abigail,	1778.	Married Noah Tyler. Is now living, 1856, at Elgin, Illinois.

These children all lived to adult years, and most of them to old age.

JOHN G. BANDELL. He was one of the fourteen thousand men, that the king of England hired of a prince of Germany, in 1775, to help subdue the rebel colonies (as was then termed) of America, that were fighting for their liberties. He came to America in 1776; was taken prisoner at the capture of Gen. Burgoyne's army, in the fall of 1777. Whether he was exchanged, or liberated on parole, or in what manner he was released is not known. He was by trade a tailor, and after leaving the army, worked both in Simsbury and Canton. In 1779 he married Sarah, daughter of Dr.

Samuel Barber, and lived some years on the side of the mountain, west of the house of Norton Case. He afterward built a house and lived some thirty years or more, on the high ground, some fifty rods west of the house of Daniel Barber; he afterward lived, and died in the house now owned by Levi, and Salmon D. Case, on the East Hill.

Parents.	Born. Died. Age.	
John G. Bandell,	1754, 1832, 78.	
Sarah Barber,	1761, 1829, 68.	
Children.	Born. Died. Age.	
Alana,	1781.	Married Grove Case.
George,	1782, 1846, 64.	
Daniel,	1784, 1832, 48.	Married Lucy Jones.
Frederick,	1786.	Married 1st, Susan Bunce; 2d, Thirza Eaton.
William,	1788.	Married Lydia Andruss.
Keturah,	1791.	Married Levi Case.
Asahel,	1794, 1834, 40.	Married Emily Carrier.
Mercy,	1796.	Married Bishop Nichols.
Samuel,	1799.	Married 1st, Amelia Hart; 2d, Thirza Russell.
Olive,	1802.	Married Levi Gridley.
Roxy,	1804.	Married Roswell Russell.
Roxanna,	1807.	Married Eli Case.

EPHRIAM BUEL, JUN. He with his wife Mercy, a sister of Samuel Barber, came from Old Simsbury, about 1743, and settled on land adjoining their brother Thomas. Their house was on the west side of Cherries brook near the west end of the saw-mill, built by Humphrey & Brown. They both died near the same time not far from 1745. The farm was then rented to Ichabod Miller, who occupied it from twelve to eighteen years. They left two little daughters, orphans. Mindwell, the oldest of them, afterward became the wife of Roger Case. The youngest of them died in childhood, leaving valuable landed property for the surviving heiress.

Children.	Born. Died. Age.
Mindwell,	1741, 1804, 63.
Mary,	1743, 1745.

PETER CURTIS, with his wife, settled in West Simsbury, about 1744, on lands now owned by Ezekiel Hosford, at a place then called Onion brook.

Parents.	Born. Died. Age.	
Peter Curtis,	1712, 1756, 44.	
Miss —— Parker.		She came from Wallingford.

Children.	Born. Died. Age.	
Israel,		He died in the army.
Eliphalet,	1734, 1806, 72.	Married Margaret Dyer.
Lucy,	1739, 1816, 77.	Married Col. Amasa Mills.
		Married Sylvanus Wilcox.
Athildred,	1745, 1805, 60.	Married Eli Case.
Peter, 2d.		
Amreth,		Married Bigelow Lawrence.
Gideon,	1751, 1789, 38.	Married Betsy Mills.
Prudence,		Married Joshua Woodruff.
Charles.		
Solomon,	1754, 1777, 23.	Died of small-pox.

Peter Curtis was the first adult person buried in the North burying-ground.

CAPT. ELIPHALET CURTIS, was the second son of Peter Curtis. He resided on the premises left him by his father. The farm is now owned by Gen. Ezekiel Hosford. He removed to western New York in the year 1800, where he died in 1806, aged about 70 years.

He married Margaret, daughter of Benjamin Dyer, who survived him a number of years, and died in the year 1812, in the stone house now owned by Lester Mather.

Children.	Born. Died. Age.	
Eliphalet, Jun.,	1758, 1816, 58.	Married 1st, Mary Wilcox; 2d, Mrs. Holcomb.
Margaret,	1760, 1798, 38.	Died single.
Thedosia.		Married 1st, Zebina Moses; 2d, Benajah Holcomb, Jun.
Chrastina.		Married Soloman Woodruff.
Narcissa.		Married Joseph Olcott.
Agnes.		Married Soloman Dill, Jun.
Horace,	1771.	Married Chloe Poison.
Gad,	1774, 1853, 79.	Married 1st, Eunice Porter; 2d, Cherissa Wilcox.
Israel.		
Sarah,	1780, 1785, 5.	Died in childhood.

Capt. Curtis was an officer in the revolutionary army in the first years of the war.

MAJ. ISRAEL CURTIS, oldest son of Peter Curtis, Sen., married Elizabeth Andrus. In his early married state he resided in the near vicinity of his father's house. They buried one child named Elizabeth; he had a son named Zebina, afterward became of notoriety in Windsor, Vermont. He removed to Windsor, Vermont, sometime previous to the commencement of the Revolutionary war, and died a major in the northern army.

MAJ. PETER CURTIS, third son of Peter Curtis, Sen., settled in Farmington; was an officer in the American army of the Revolution; was after the war a brigade major and also a major in the line. He was the first keeper of Newgate prison, in Granby, commencing 1790, and left it in 1796, in declining health, and died in 1797. He had two sons Jeptha and Adna, and two daughters. Betsey and Nancy.

GIDEON CURTIS, was the 4th son of Peter Curtis, Sen. He married Elizabeth or Betsey, daughter of Rev. Gideon Mills. He resided on the premises, and built the house now standing some forty rods north-east from Gen. Ezekiel Hosford's. He was by occupation a blacksmith. He, by an overlifting in his youthful days, brought on a disease or weakness of the back, which caused him to endure frequent spells of sickness and suffering by turns through his remaining years, and brought him down to the grave in 1789. Several circumstances and traits of character in this excellent man, and his amiable companion, are thought worthy of notice in this short sketch of a few things respecting them. They were both, in their natural turn and deportment uncommonly kind and agreeable, but beyond this, they both exhibited those good properties that go to show what divine grace can raise some of our human race to be in the humbler walks of life. They both, to an eminent degree manifested Christian resignation under adversity, which, at the same time was at a great remove from unfeeling indifference. Some things respecting Mr. Curtis will here be noticed. He was troubled with stammering in his speech, to an uncommon degree. He was a singer of the first order. His voice and scientific accomplishments would compare well among the first masters and teachers of that time, though his knowledge and his high attainments, were produced by his own native musical genius, aided by his own application to the science as he had opportunity.

His impediment in speech was no embarrassment in his singing except in mentioning tunes, and occasional speaking, and his vital strength held out to within a short time of his death. His weakness, and spinal sensitiveness was such that for many weeks he required to be lifted from his bed to his chair, and even to be turned from side to side on his bed, yet he could join with his friends and attendants who loved singing, and would occasionally favor them by singing some European or American set pieces, which he had in his mental store, consisting of music from Madan, and others. He would often sing the anthem from 7th of Job, music by

Lyons, and remark at the close, that it was applicable to his own case; he loved to sing the Dying Christian, music by Billings. Having sold the place on which he commenced his family state, he lived his last year in a house then standing the west side of the road, opposite the house of James Humphrey, and died there. He was viewed by Christian people as one who could understandingly confide in the rectitude of God's dealings with him. The same traits of character were seen to adorn the life of his worthy partner, both during his life, and through the remainder of her life, which closed in A.D. 1825. She, for the last twenty-seven years of her life, was the wife of the Rev. Rufus Hawley, of Northington, (now Avon.) It appeared to be a settled principle with her, that whatsoever God did was right. They were the parents of six children.

Parents.	Born.	Died.	Age.
Gideon Curtis,	1751,	1789,	38.
Elizabeth (or Betsey) Mills,	1753,	1825,	72.

Children.	Born.	Died.	Age.	
Child,	1774,	1774.		
Gideon, 2d,	1775.			Married an adopted daughter of Capt. Sweet, of Norfolk.
Solomon,	1778.			Married a daughter of Samuel Eggleston.
Drayton Mills,	1781.			Married a lady educated by the Moravians.
Norman,	1785.			He was a stammerer.
Elizabeth, or Betsey,	1788.			Married Thomas Gleason, of Avon.

These families that bore the name of Curtis were among the most prominent in West Simsbury, the later part of the last century, although the race has now become almost extinct in this town, and but very few are now living that had any knowledge of them.

SERG. DANIEL CASE, 2D. He removed from the old parish to West Simsbury about the year 1746 or 47, accompanied by his three brothers, Dudley, Zacheus, and Ezekiel, and two sisters, Mindwell, wife of David Adams, and Lois, wife of Joseph Mills, Jun. He resided on the premises now occupied by Calvin Case.

Parents.	Born. Died. Age.	
Daniel Case,	1720, 1801, 81.	
Mary Watson,	1724, 1807, 83.	Of New Hartford.

Children.	Born. Died. Age.	
Daniel,	1752, 1799, 47.	Married Elizabeth Humphrey.
Moses,	1754, 1782, 28.	Married Eunice Case.
Mary,	1756, 1832. 76.	Married John Garret.
Abigail,	1758, 1830, 72.	Married William Taylor.
Lois,	1760.	Died single.
Keturah,	1762, 1824, 62.	Married James Humphrey, Esq.
Penlope,	1764, 1781, 17.	Died single.
Amery Watson,	1767, 1852, 85.	Married Betsey Hawes.
Elam,	1772, 1848. 76.	Married Phebe Andrus, widow of Leman Andrus.

Mr. Daniel Case, erected the first grist-mill in West Simsbury, on the site now occupied by Calvin Case, Jun., and Orange Case.

SERG. DANIEL CASE, 1ST, married Penlope Buttolph, May 7th, 1719; died May 28th, 1733, aged 37 years.

LIEUT. DANIEL CASE, son of Serg. Daniel Case, 2d, married Elizabeth, daughter of Capt. Ezekiel Humphrey, Sen., about A. D. 1771. They resided on the farm now owned by Stephen H. Atwater.

Parents.	Born. Died. Age.	
Daniel Case,	1752, 1799, 47.	
Elizabeth Humphrey,	1750, 1808, 58.	

Children.	Born. Died. Age.	
Nancy,	1772.	
Daniel,	1774.	
Harvey,	1777.	
Moses,	1779.	
Penlope.		
Hugh.		Was killed by the bursting of a cask of burning spirits, 1800.
Ruel.		

The children removed to the state of New York, at the beginning of this century.

OZIAS CASE, son of Lieut. Dudley Case. He resided the early part of his family state in the near vicinity of the house of Dea. Lester Mather; there he lost one or more of the early members of his family. About 1791 he removed to Otis, Mass., where he spent the remainder of his life.

Parents.	Born. Died. Age.	
Ozias Case,	1757, 1820, 63.	
Mary Hill,	1804.	
Amy Baldwin,	1811.	

Children.	Born. Died. Age.	
Mary, or Polly,	1774.	Married Charles Segar.
Ozias, Jun.,	1776.	Married Esther D'Wolf.
Manna,	1779.	Married Electa Barber.
Dorcas.		
Luman.		Married ——— Humphrey.
George,	1790.	
Dencey,	1792.	Married 1st, Thomas Bidwell, Jun.; 2d, Amos Rising.
Dudley.		

LIEUT. DUDLEY CASE. He removed from the old parish to West Simsbury, about the year 1742. He resided on the place known as the Hosford Stand, where he kept public house for a long succession of years.

Parents.	Born. Died. Age.
Dudley Case,	1722, 1792, 70.
Dorcas Humphrey,	1726, 1805, 79.

Children.	Born. Died. Age.	
Dudley,	1744, 1822, 78.	Married 1st, Susannah Merrell; 2d, Lucretia Case.
Elisha,	1747.	Died in youth.
Ozias,	1749.	Died in youth.
Elias,	1753.	Died in youth.
Elisha,	1755, 1839, 84.	Married Delight Griswold.
Ozias,	1757.	Married Mary Hills.
Elias,	1759, 1809, 50.	Married Lucretia Foot.
Dan,	1761, 1815, 54.	Married 1st, Rachel Foot; 2d, Allice Hallock.
Dorcas,	1764, 1849, 85.	Married 1st, Benjamin Mills; 2d, Nodiah Woodruff.
Truman,	1767, 1836, 69.	Married Rhoda Lusk.
Emmanuel,	1769, 1782, 13.	

They had eleven children, ten sons and one daughter.

CAPT. DUDLEY CASE, JUN., son of Lieut. Dudley Case, married Susannah, daughter of Jonathan Merrell, Sen. He resided on the premises now owned by the heirs of the late Hiram Pike, near the confines of New Hartford. They had no children. For his second wife, he married Lucretia, relict of Capt. Elias Case. He was born in 1744; died 1822, aged 78 years. His first wife, Susannah, died 1810. Lucretia, his second wife, died 1843.

DEA. **ELISHA CASE**, fifth son of Lieut. Dudley Case, grandson of Daniel Case, Sen., and of the fifth degree inclusive from the first John Case. He resided on the premises now occupied by Newell Miner.

Parents.	Born. Died. Age.	
Elisha Case,	1755, 1839, 84.	
Delight Griswold,	1757, 1842, 85.	Daughter of Samuel Griswold.

Children.	Born. Died. Age.	
Almira,	1777, 1808, 31.	Married David Wilmot.
Sally,	1779, 1846, 67.	Married Thaddeus, son of Dea. Benjamin Mills.
Elisha,	1781, 1824, 48.	Married Abia Barber, daughter of John Barber.
Delight G.,	1783, 1810, 27.	Married John Barber, 2d.
Allen,	1785, 1849, 64.	Married 1st, Sally, daughter of Obed Higley; 2d, Catharine, daughter of Phineas Squires.
Zulima,	1787, 1802, 15.	
Erastus,	1789.	Married Mary, daughter of Col. Theodore Pettibone.
Electa,	1791.	Married Reuben Hill.
Harvey,	1793, 1853, 60.	Married Amelia, daughter of Col. Arnold Humphrey.
Fanny,	1796, 1796.	
John,	1797, 1854, 57.	Married Susan, daughter of Maj. Gad Frisbie.
Emily,	1799.	Married Lemuel Whitman.
Fanny,	1802.	Married 1st, Tracy Humphrey; 2d, —— Hurlbut.
Edmund,	1806, 1848, 42.	Married 1st, Nancy C. Hinman; 2d, Harriet R. King.

DEA. **ABRAHAM CASE**, son of Bartholomew and Mary, daughter of Ensign Samuel Humphrey, married 1699.

He, with his brother Amos, removed from the old society about the year 1740. He resided on the East Hill, on the premises occupied by the heirs of his grandson, Lyman Case, deceased. He had nine children, two sons and seven daughters; all were married and had children except Abraham and Rachel. It is proper to state here that for a great number of years the East Hill went by the name of Chestnut Hill. The appellation now given to it is of more recent date.

Parents.	Born.	Died.	Age.	
Abraham Case,	1720,	1800,	80.	
1st wife, Rachel Case,	1722,	1790.		Sister of Capt. Josiah Case.
2d, widow Webster,	1727.			

Children.	Born.	Died.	Age.	
Rachel,	1741,	1759,	18.	
Abraham, Jun.,	1743,	1776,	33.	Married Sarah Humphrey.
Rosanna,	1745,	1807,	62.	Married Ezra Wilcox.
Elisha,	1747,	1808,	61.	Married 1st, Judith Case; 2d, Elizabeth Case.
Sarah,	1752,	1781,	30.	Married Caleb Case.
Eunice,	1753.			Married 1st, Moses Case; 2d, Ebenezer Cowles.
Hannah,	1755,	1808,	53.	Married Charles Humphrey.
Elizabeth,	1757,	1836,	79.	Married Giles Humphrey.
Phebe,	1759,	1798,	54.	Married Jeremy Griswold.

ABRAHAM CASE, Jun., married Sarah, oldest daughter of Oliver Humphrey, Esq. They resided on what was called the Fowler farm, situated north of Collinsville, and now belongs to the farm of Addison O. Mills. They left no children. He died about 1776; his widow afterward married to Rev. Abraham Fowler, and by him, had one son, born 1784, named Abraham Case Fowler.

Capt. ELISHA CASE, son of Dea. Abraham Case, married Judith, daughter of Jeremiah or Jeremy Case. He resided on the farm left by his father and father-in-law. They, during their family state, had seven children, four of whom (the two first and two last) sunk into idiocy and died in early youth. Three of them lived to adult years, settled in family state and had children.

Parents.	Born. Died. Age.	
Elisha Case,	1747, 1808, 61.	
Judith Case,	1749, 1805, 56.	

Children that grew up.	Born. Died. Age.	
Grove,	1773.	Married Alana Bandell.
Roxy,	1776, 1811, 35.	Married 1st, William McFarland; 2d, William Wilcox, Jun.
Lyman,	1778, 1832, 54.	

AMOS CASE, brother of Abraham Case, removed from the old parish to West Simsbury, about the year 1740.

They were sons of Bartholomew and Mary, daughter of Ensign Samuel Humphrey, who were married in the year 1699.

He resided on the East Hill, in the house lately occupied by Abel Case, and now occupied by Myron Case.

They had ten children, five sons and five daughters, who all lived to adult years, and all left children, except Seth and Lucy.

Parents.	Born. Died. Age.	
Amos Case,	1712, 1798, 86.	Married, 1739.
Mary Holcomb,	1714, 1802, 88.	

Children.	Born. Died. Age.	
Mary,	1739, 1834, 95.	Married Simeon Case, son of Richard Case, 2d.
Ruth,	1742, 1794, 52.	Married Richard Case, son of Richard Case, 2d.

Huldah,	1744, 1774, 30.	Died single.
Amos,	1746, 1798, 52.	Married Betsey Ward.
Abel,	1748, 1834, 86.	Married 1st, Huldah Higley; 2d, Lucy Perry.
Silas,	1749, 1809, 59.	Married 1st, Jane Kelly: 2d, Mary Case.
Lucy,	1752, 1837, 85.	Married 1st, Ruggles Humphrey; 2d, Solomon Buel.
Pliney,	1754, 1780, 26.	Married Rhoda Merrell.
Rhoda,	1757, 1786, 29.	Married Hosea Case, 2d.
Seth,	1760, 1776, 16.	Died single.

Seth, the youngest son, died in the American army, near New York, in 1776, and although his brothers, Abel and Silas, were there at the same time, they were not allowed by their officers to see him during his sickness.

ABEL CASE, SEN., second son of Amos Case, Sen., married Huldah Higley, daughter of the second Brewster Higley. He resided through life on the premises that were previously occupied by his father, in the East Hill school district.

Parents.	Born. Died. Age.	
Abel Case, Sen.,	1748, 1834, 86.	Married, 1777.
1st wife, Huldah Higley,	1750, 1810, 60.	
2d wife, Lucy Perry.	1815.	

Children.	Born. Died. Age.	
Huldah,	1778.	Married Jabez Hamblin; he died 1834, aged 56.
Abel, Jun.,	1783, 1831, 48.	Married Rachel Humphrey.
Dinah,	1786, 1848, 62.	Married Ira Case.
Tirzah,	1787.	Married Sadoce Case.
Carmi,	1793, 1815, 22.	

SILAS CASE. third son of Amos Case, Sen.

Parents.	Born. Died. Age.
Silas Case,	1749, 1809, 59.
1st wife, Jane Kelly,	1777.
2d wife, Mary Case,	1755, 1833, 74.

Children.	Born. Died. Age.	
Kelly,	1777.	Married 1st, Roxy Hoskins; 2d, Mabel Steele.
Polly,	1781, 1850, 69.	Married Giles Case.
Ira,	1782, 1848, 66.	Married Mary Humphrey, and Dinah Case.
Silas, Jun.,	1785, 1816, 31.	
Levi,	1787.	Married Keturah Bandell.
Ruggles,	1789.	Married Cynthia Case.
Jane,	1792.	Married Holcomb Case.
Lucy,	1794.	Married Everest Case.
Gad,	1796.	Married Tirzah Gibbons.
Ruth,	1799, 1832, 33.	Married Case Braman.

SERG. RICHARD CASE, 2D. He was son of Capt. Richard, and grandson of the first John Case. He removed to West Simsbury in 1737, and is supposed to have been the first settler, and to have erected the first dwelling-house in this portion of the town. His son Sylvanus has ever been reputed to have been the first English child born within the limits of West Simsbury. He resided on the East Hill; the building-site is still to be seen opposite the dwelling-house lately erected by his great grandson, John Case, Esq.

Parents.	Born. Died. Age.
Richard Case,	1710, 1769, 59.
Mercy Holcomb,	1712, 1780, 68.

Children.	Born. Died. Age.	
Richard, 3d	1734, 1805, 71.	Married Ruth Case.
Joab,	1735, 1758, 4.	

Sylvanus,	1737, 1817, 80.	Married 1st, Caroline Humphrey; 2d, widow Hepzibah Humphrey; she died, 1818, aged 74.
Simeon,	1739, 1822, 83.	Married Mary Case.
Eli,	1741, 1804, 62.	Married Athildred Curtis.
Uriah,	1743, 1826, 83.	Married 1st, Susannah Lawrence; 2d, Eunice Dill.
Edward,	1748, 1822, 75.	Married Zeruah Lawrence.
Phineas,	1750, 1798, 48.	Married Sarah Tuller.
Mercy,	1752, 1818, 66.	Married Abram Moses.
Naoma,	1755, 1822, 66.	Married David Pettibone.
Timothy,	1759, 1850, 92.	Married Esther Brown.

In this family of eleven children they all lived to adult years, and married, except Joab.

SYLVANUS CASE, third son of Richard Case, 2d. He lived about forty rods, north of the present site of the East Hill school-house; the site now belongs to Theron Case.

Parents.	Born. Died. Age.	
Sylvanus Case,	1737, 1817, 80.	
1st wife, Caroline Humphrey.		Widow of Benajah Humphrey.
2d wife, Hepzibah Humphrey.	1743, 1817, 74.	Widow of William Humphrey.

Children.	Born. Died. Age.	
Caroline,	1776.	Married Allen Woodruff, of Farmington.
Sylvanus, 2d.,	1778, 1806, 28.	Dropped dead while working in the field.
Hepzibah.		Married David Latimer, of Simsbury.
Rufus.		Married Polly Dibble, of Southwick.

CAPT. URIAH CASE, son of Serg. Richard Case, 2d. He resided on the farm left by his father on the East Hill. For his first wife he married Susan Lawrence; 2d, Eunice Dill; 3d, Mary Case, widow of Silas Case. He had four children by his first wife, and eleven by his second. He died 1826, aged 83. His wife died 1815, aged 61.

Children.	Born. Died. Age.	
Zilpah,	1766,	Married Isaiah Taylor.
Sylvia,	1768.	Married 1st, Amasa Tuller; 2d, David Sutliff.
Uriah, Jun.,	1771.	Married Sarah Noble;* she died 1807, aged 31.
Susannah,	1774, 1808, 34.	Married Jared Mills, Jun.
Eunice,	1780.	Married Roswell Reed.
Joab,	1779, 1818, 39.	Married Sarah Case.
Watson,	1781, 1853, 72.	Married Sylvia Case.
Elizabeth,	1783, 1808, 25.	Died single.
Holcomb,	1784, 1854, 69.	Married Jane Case.
Lorinda,	1786, 1808, 22.	Died single; she and Elizabeth were both buried at the same time; they both died very near the same time of the spotted fever.
Clara, } twins,	1788.	
Laura, }	1788, 1842, 54.	Married Charles Humphrey.
Cynthia,	1793.	Married Ruggles Case.
Lydia,	1791, 1822, 31.	
Lucinda,	1796	Married Hiram Case.

ELI CASE, son of Serg. Richard Case, 2d, resided on the premises now owned by Lucian B. Case, on the East Hill.

Parents.	Born. Died. Age.
Eli Case,	1741, 1804, 62.
Athildred Curtis,	1745, 1805, 60.

---

* She was the first person interred in the burying-ground in Suffrage Village. Her death was occasioned by jumping from a waggon; a lady riding with her remained in the waggon and escaped unhurt.

Children.	Born. Died. Age.	
Athildred,	1766, 1804, 38.	Married Ephraim B. Case.
Eli, Jun.,	1768, 1795, 27.	Married Hannah Alford.
Riverius,	1770, 1822, 52.	Married Abigail Case.
Zabad,	1772, 1836, 64.	Married Sarah Merritt.
Giles,	1776, 1851, 75.	Married Mary Case.
Orange,	1779, 1814, 35.	Married Sarah Jones; was killed in falling a tree.
Thede,	1781.	Married Ozias Woodford.
Calvin,	1782.	Married 1st, Diantha Humphrey; 2d, Sarah Case.
Chastina,	1784, 1826, 42.	Married David Ackart.
Harriet,	1788, 1845, 57.	Married Trueman Allen.

It is supposed one died in infancy.

TIMOTHY CASE, son of Serg. Richard Case, 2d, grandson of Richard, 1st, and great grandson of the first John Case, with his wife, Esther, daughter of Capt. John Brown, commenced family state about 1781. They resided on the premises now owned by his grandnephew, John Case, Esq., till 1797; then removed to Otis, Mass., and lived there till 1822; they then removed to Andover, Ohio, to spend the remainder of their days. They had fourteen children.

Parents.	Born. Died. Age.	
Timothy Case,	1759, 1850, 92.	Married 1781.
Esther Brown,	1762, 1838, 76.	

Children.	Born. Died. Age.	
Infant,	1782.	
Infant,	1783.	
Esther,	1784, 1846, 62.	Married Daniel Strickland.
Flora,	1786.	Married ——— Pratt.
Timothy, Jun.,	1788, 1816, 28.	Married Roeny Brewster.
Alcy,	1789,	Married Amos Miner.
Amorett,	1791.	Married Ira Nichols.
Hannah,	1793.	Married O. Clarke.

Hiram,	1795, 1815, 20.	Died single.
Salmon,	1797, 1844, 47.	
Norman,	1799, 1822, 24.	
Selah,	1801.	
Orren,	1803, 1803.	
Orren Brown,	1804.	

PHINEAS CASE, son of Serg. Richard Case, 2d, with his wife, lived in West Granby, near by his brother Richard, till about 1792, when he moved on to the place, which is the east part of the farm of Israel W. Graham, where he resided through life.

Parents.	Born. Died. Age.
Phineas Case,	1750, 1798, 48.
Sarah Tuller.	

Children.	Born. Died. Age.	
Sally.		Married James Ross.
Lovisa.		
Mercy.		Married Edgar Taylor.
Rosella.		Married Edmund Miner.
Amorett.		
Phineas, Jun.		Married Sally Beckwith.
Leman,		

It appears by burial-record, they lost an infant in 1781; one in 1782, and one in 1794.

LIEUT. RICHARD CASE, or Richard 3d, oldest son of Serg. Richard, 2d, and Mercy Case, married Ruth, daughter of Amos Case, Sen., about 1756. He resided on the farm, and erected the dwelling-house lately owned by the members of the Jacob Edgerton family, in West Granby.

Parents.	Born. Died. Age.
Richard Case, 3d,	1734, 1805, 71.
1st wife, Ruth Case,	1741, 1794, 53.
2d wife, Mary Case,	1732, 1817, 85.

Children.	Born. Died. Age.	
Richard, Jun., or 4th,	1757.	Married Jemima Moore.
Ruth,	1759, 1854, 95.	Married Moses Miller.
George.		Married Lucy Hayes.
Jemima.		Married Oliver Case.
Japhet,	1766, 1809, 43.	Married Chloe Thrall.
Starling.		Married Isabel Wilcox.
Apphia,	1772, 1796, 24.	
Huldah,	1774, 1794, 21.	
Chauncey,	1777.	Married Cleopatra Hayes.
Gideon,	1779, 1849, 70.	Married Temperance Miner.
Cyrus,	1781.	Married Abigail Couch.
Olive,	1783.	Married Noah Case, 3d.
Freeman,	1789.	Married Sybil Bliss.

SIMEON CASE, son of Serg. Richard Case, 2d, with his wife Mary, daughter of Amos Case, Sen., settled in family state, about 1759. They resided on the premises that were owned by the heirs of the late Francis Case, in West Granby.

Parents.	Born. Died. Age.
Simeon Case,	1739, 1823, 84.
Mary Case,	1739, 1826, 86.

Children.	Born. Died. Age.	
Simeon, Jun.,	1756, 1819, 57.	Married Phebe Burr.
Titus,	1764, 1816, 51.	Married Amy Reed.
Mary,	1771, 1821, 50.	
Obed,	1765, 1849, 84.	Married Rachel Emmons.
Eliphalet,	1770, 1847, 77.	Married Rachel Case; died 1813, aged 46.
Ashbel,	1762, 1816, 44.	Married Polly Frazier.

Alexander,	1774, 1824, 50.	Married Mindwell Case; died 1830, aged 51.
Francis,	1777, 1845, 68.	Married Jemima Case.
Robert,	1780,	Married Clarrissa Case.
Peter.		
Elizabeth.		Married Reuben Russell.

CAPT. JOSIAH CASE. He was son of James Case and Esther Fithen. He removed from the old parish to West Simsbury about the year 1743. He resided on the premises now occupied by his grandson, Gen. Jarvis Case, Esq., on Chestnut Hill.

Parents.	Born. Died. Age.	
Josiah Case,	1717, 1789, 72.	
Hestor Higley,	1719, 1807, 88.	

Children.	Born. Died. Age.	
Lois,	1741, 1759, 18.	
James,	1743, 1820, 77.	Married 1st, Phebe Tuller; 2d, Lydia Case.
Hestor,	1745, 1790, 45.	Married 1st, Thomas Case; 2d, Carmi Higley; 3d, Abram Pinney.
Hannah,	1750, 1833, 83.	Married Amos Wilcox.
Betty,	1752, 1817, 63.	Married John Barber.
Fithen,	1758, 1829, 77.	Married Amarila Humphrey.

JEREMY CASE, son of Capt. James Case. He, with his wife Judith, came from Simsbury about the year 1745. He settled on the place now owned by the family of the late David Ackart, deceased. He had as far as is known three children.

Children.	Born. Died. Age.	
Jeremy,	1746.	Married to a Miss Phelps.
William,	1751.	Married Sarah Hicox.
Judith,	1749, 1805, 56.	Married Elisha Case.

CAPT. FITHIN CASE, second son of Capt. Josiah Case settled where his son, Gen. Jarvis Case, now lives. In this family of eleven children they all lived to settle in family state except Salma.

Parents.	Born. Died. Age.
Fithin Case,	1758, 1829. 71.
Amarilla Humphrey,	1764, 1845, 81.

Children.	Born. Died. Age.	
Mariah,	1781, 1856, 75.	Married Moses Case, son of Lieut. Moses Case; died 1850, aged 75.
Fithin, Jun.,	1784, 1853, 69.	Married Statira Phelps.
Mamre,	1786.	Married Abia Tuller.
Amarilla,	1788.	Married Chauncey Eno.
Josiah, W.,	1790, 1830, 40.	Married Agnes Case.
Salma,	1792, 1794, 2.	
Lavinia Charity,	1794.	Married Col. Salmon Merrell.
Jasper,	1796.	Married Flora Humphrey.
Melissa,	1799.	2d wife of Ithuel Gridley.
Jarvis,	1801.	Married Lucia Adams.
Julia,	1805, 1845, 40.	1st wife of Ithuel Gridley.

DEA. HOSEA CASE. He removed from the old parish to West Simsbury, about the year 1752.

He resided on the hill, east of Isaac Tuller's, now Augustus H. Carrier's.

They had eleven children; four sons and seven daughters; all were married except Dorcas, and nine of them left descendants.

Parents.	Born. Died. Age.
Hosea Case,	1793.
Mary Case,	1817.

Children.	Born. Died. Age.	
Mary,	1752.	Married John Hill, of Burlington.

Elizabeth,	1753, 1839, 86.	Married Reuben Barber.
Hosea,	1756, 1834, 78.	Married 1st, Rhoda Case; 2d. Sarah Buel.
Asa,	1758, 1837, 78.	Married 1st, Lois Dill; 2d, Thede Humphrey.
Lydia,	1761.	Married Benjamin Barber.
Dosa,	1763, 1778, 15.	Died in single life.
Rosanna,	1766, 1839, 73.	Married Peter Frederick Buel.
Titus,	1768, 1845, 76.	Married 1st, Rebecca Eggleston; 2d, Phebe Tuttle.
Eunice,	1770.	Married Arba Alford.
Lodama,	1774.	Married Aaron Case.
Phebe,	1776, 1745, 69.	Married 1st, Leman Andrus; 2d, Elam Case.

CAPT. ZACHEUS CASE, brother of Daniel, Dudley and Ezekiel, removed from Meadow-plain, old parish, to West Simsbury, about the year 1746, or 47.

He resided on the premises now occupied by Ephraim Mills, Esq.

He with his wife, and their son Caleb, removed to Whitestown, New York, in 1792.

Parents.	Born. Died. Age.
Zacheus Case,	1728, 1812, 84.
Abigail Barber,	1730, 1798, 68.

Children.	Born. Died. Age.	
Caleb,	1754.	Married 2d, Sarah Case; 3d, Rhoda Case.
Zacheus,	1757.	Died in youth.
Abigail,	1759.	Married Charles Wilcox.
Mary,	1761, 1809, 48.	Married Col. William Wilcox.
Sarah,	1764, 1830, 66.	Married 1st, Jedediah Wilcox; 2d, Frederick Humphrey; 3d, Wait Munson.
Thede,	1766, 1851. 86.	Married 1st, Benajah Humphrey; 2d, Asa Case.
Rhoda,	1768. 1798, 30.	Married Caina Mills.
Ruth,	1770, 1809, 39.	Married Daniel Alburtson.

CALEB CASE, son of Capt. Zacheus and Abigail Case, erected the house now owned by Plinny Case, and resided in it during part of his family state in Canton.

Parents.	Born. Died. Age.	
Caleb Case,	1754.	
1st wife, Sarah Case	1751, 1781, 30.	Daughter of Dea. Abraham Case.
2d wife, Rhoda Case,	1757, 1792, 35.	Widow of Plinny Case.

Children.	Born. Died. Age.	
Horris,	1776.	Married Sarah, daughter of William Case.
Betsey,	1778.	
Sarah,	1780,	Married 1st, Joab Case; 2d, Absalom Graham.
Zacheus,	1787.	
Philemon,	1788.	
Rhoda,	1792.	

NOAH CASE, Sen., second son of John Case, 3d. He resided about half a mile north-west of where Wells Wilcox now lives in the south-west corner of Granby. He was brother to Capt. John, Job, Charles and Lucy, and grandfather of Noah, Abner and Anson.

Parents.	Born. Died. Age.
Noah Case,	1720, 1797, 77.
Myriam Holcomb,	1720, 1795, 75.

Children.	Born. Died. Age.	
Noah, 2d,	1741, 1807, 66.	Married Mary, daughter of Lieut. David Adams.
Amy,	1744.	Married Titus Reed.
Myriam,	1746, 1750, 14.	
Roger,	1748.	
Abner,	1752, 1807, 55.	Married Hannah Case.

Ruth,	1754.	
Darius,	1756, 1801, 45.	Married Mary Giddings.
Lydia,	1758,	Married James Case.

DARIUS CASE, fourth son of Noah Case, Sen., resided on the place now owned by his son Anson Case.

Parents.	Born. Died. Age.	
Darius Case,	1756, 1801, 46.	Married, 1782.
Mary Giddings.		

Children.	Born. Died. Age.	
Darius, 2d,	1783.	Married Dilla Barber.
Clarrissa,	1784, 1827, 43.	1st wife of Robert Case.
Harriet,	1786.	Married Warren Emmons.
Tempa,	1789.	Married 1st, Zacheus Wilcox; 2d, Amos Tuller.
Anson,	1791.	Married Rachel Case.
Laura,	1793, 1849, 56.	Married William Colt.
Austin,	1795.	
Rosadile,	1797, 1855, 58.	Married Abiel Case.

The daughter Laura, with her husband, were both killed by an accident on a railroad in the State of New Hampshire, about six years since.

EZEKIEL CASE, Sen., a brother of Daniel and Dudley. He removed from the old parish to West Simsbury, about the year 1754, and settled on the premises now owned by Stephen H. Atwater.

Parents.	Born. Died. Age,	
Ezekiel Case,	1731.	
1st wife, LucyCornish,	1770.	
2d wife, Mary Hoskins,		Married 1771.

Children by 1st wife.	Born, Died, Age.	
Lucy,	1754, 1777, 23.	1st wife of Solomon Humphrey.
Ezekiel, 2d,	1756.	

Violet,	1758.	Married Asa Gillet.
Frederick,	1761.	
Abigail,	1763.	
Rachel,	1766.	
Benoni,	1769.	

Child by 2d wife.	Born. Died. Age.
Abijah,	1771.

Some incidents in the history of Ezekiel Case, 2d, may be mentioned here. He was in the American army in 1776, and for the crime of deserting to the British army, he was sentenced to death, but was reprieved and pardoned, by the interposition of Elisha Cornish, Sen. In 1793, he was brought to capital trial for killing a child of Mr. Aikley, of Bloomfield, but was acquitted of murder on the ground of insanity.

JACOB CASE, 1st, born 1699, died 1763, aged 64.

Abigail Barber, born 1702, died 1779, aged 77.

JACOB CASE, 2d, son of Jacob and Abigail Case, came to West Simsbury about 1760. He settled on the place now owned by his granddaughter, widow Godard. They had three children, one son and two daughters.

Parents.	Born. Died. Age.	
Jacob Case, 2d,	1735, 1807, 72.	He hung himself in his owh barn.
Elizabeth Hokins,	1804.	

Children.	Born. Died, Age.	
Betsey,	1831.	Married Jehiel Lattimer.
Mary,		Married Abraham Humphrey.
Jacob.		Died in youth.

JESSE CASE, son of Jacob Case the first, (who was a descendant of Joseph Case,) settled in West Simsbury about the year 1763, and lived on the place afterward owned by his son the late Augustus Case, deceased.

Parents.	Born. Died. Age.	
Jesse Case, Sen.,	1738, 1807, 69.	
Sarah Humphrey.		Daughter of Capt. Noah Humphrey.

Children.	Born. Died. Age.	
Jesse, Jun.,	1767, 1842, 75.	Married Sarah Cornish and Lydia Church.
Sarah,	1768.	Married Samuel Leet.
Augustus,	1770, 1855, 85.	Married Hannah Hoskins.
Abigail,	1774, 1825, 49.	Married Riverius Case.
Aseneth, 1st,	1772, 1776, 4.	Died single.
Aseneth, 2d,	1777, 1845, 68.	
Gideon,	1779, 1822, 39.	Married Persis Seward.
Hannah,	1781.	Married Edmund O. Sullivan.
Charlotte,	1785.	Married Allen Barber, of Windsor.
Saloma,	1786, 1787, 1.	

DEA. JESSE CASE, first son of Jesse Case, Sen., resided near the paternal homestead, now the residence of Jesse O. Case, in the Farms District, Canton, formerly West Simsbury. The old paternal homestead where he was born, was the first house built in that section of the town, and stood upon the side hill about one hundred rods north-west of his late residence. The house in which he lived and died, was built by him about the year 1800.

Parents.	Born. Died. Age
Jesse Case,	1767, 1842, 75.
1st wife, Sarah Cornish,	1773, 1815, 42.
2d wife, Lydia Church,	1778.

Children by 1st wife.	Born. Died. Age.	
Jessie O.,	1792,	Married Chloe Gleason.
Justin,	1795, 1802.	
Everest	1796.	Married Lucy Case.
Sarah,	1798.	Married Ezekiel H. Wilcox.
Newton,	1801, 1807.	
Elmina,	1803.	
Justin	1805, 1841, 36.	Married Rachel H. Talcott.
Newton,	1807.	Married Lemira B. Hurlburt.
Rowena,	1809, 1834, 25.	
Abigail,	1812.	

Children by 2d wife.	Born. Died. Age.
Lydia C.,	1817, 1820, 3.
Lydia,	1820.

JOSIAH CLARKE. He lived and died on the place now owned by Robert Wilcox. He commenced about 1748. Mr. Clarke and several of his family, were cut down in quick succession by a fever of a very malignant type; three of his family were interred in succession in the North burying-ground, 1779.

Parents.	Born. Died. Age.	
Josiah Clarke,	1727, 1777, 50.	
Deliverance,	1728, 1801, 73.	She was the third wife of John Segar.

Children.	Born. Died. Age.	
Josiah,	1753, 1821, 68,	Married Zilde ——.
Deliverance,	1751, 1779, 28.	Married John F. Frasier.
Susannah,	1761, 1779, 18.	
Elihu,	1763, 1779, 16.	
Timothy,	1768.	Married Rachel Gilbert.

Of the other members of this family, the compiler has no knowledge.

MR. ——— CLARKE. He, with his wife and children, settled on the farm now known by the name of the Cook farm, on Bald Hill, about the year 1743.

He, with two or three of his sons, were cut down by a violent fever, which deprived the family of its help, about A. D. 1754.

The family soon left the place, and it afterward came into the hands of Isaac Graham, who lived on it through his lifetime.

But little is known of the family.

THOMAS CAVERLEE, married Sarah, daughter of Isaac and Sarah Graham, and resided for many years, at the corner of the old roads, some sixty rods east of his father Graham's house, on Bald Hill; Mr. Caverlee's house stood near the north-east corner of the lot, south of the road on land now belonging to Gideon M. Case. After 1800, he resided at different places. He was a soldier of the Revolution, but died before the pension law was enacted, so that he, with many others died poor, without having received any just compensation for their services and suffering in their country's cause.

Parents.	Born.	Died.	Age.
Thomas Caverlee,	1752,	1815,	63.
Sarah Graham.			

Children.	Born.	Died.	Age.	
Thomas, Jun,,	1781,	1781.		
Thomas, 2d,	1782.			Married Mary Ann ———.
Sarah,	1784.			Married ——— Buel.
Melinda,	1786			Married Jonathan Medar, who died in New York, 1830.
Cromwell,	1788.			
Britta,	1794,	1824,	30.	

BENJAMIN DYER. He was a schoolmate of the renowned Dr. Benjamin Franklin. He removed with his wife from Boston to Hartford, 1735, and in the year 1745, removed and settled in West Simsbury, on land now owned by Luther Higley, Esq., near the south end of what is claimed to belong to the parsonage grant. He was by trade a tallow chandler.

Parents.	Born. Died. Age.	
Benjamin Dyer,	1701, 1775, 74.	Born in Boston.
Margaret Clap.		

Children.	Born. Died. Age.	
Thomas,	1728, 1803, 75.	Married Azubah Humphrey.
Mary.		Married Elisha Cornish.
Benjamin, 1st,	1746.	Died in youth.
Joseph.		Died in the French War.
Margaret,	1738, 1812. 74.	Married Eliphalet Curtis.
John.	1793.	Died single.
Sarah,		Married 1st, John Hutchinson; 2d, Mr. Edson.
Hannah.		Married Benjamin Adams.
Benjamin, 2d,	1747, 1815, 68.	Married Anna Northway.
Daniel,	1749, 1814, 64.	Married Sarah Northway.

The second Benjamin was born November, 1747, in the house now occupied by Luther Higley, Esq., which shows that house to have been built 109 years.

LIEUT. BENJAMIN DYER, son of Benjamin and Margaret Dyer, married Anna Northway, a sister to brother Daniel's wife. He resided most of his life, with his brother Daniel, and their farms were adjoining and interwoven in some measure with each other.

Parents.	Born. Died. Age.
Benjamin Dyer,	1747.
Anna Northway,	1752, 1843, 91.

Child.	Born. Died. Age.	
Ralph,	1782, 1841, 59.	Married Achsah Bidwell; she died December 25, 1840.

THOMAS DYER, son of Benjamin and Margaret Dyer, resided on land adjoining his father. He commenced about the year 1756. He married Azubah, daughter of Samuel Humphrey, 3d.

Parents.	Born. Died. Age.
Thomas Dyer,	1729, 1803, 74.
Azubah Humphrey,	1737, 1816, 79.

Children.	Born. Died. Age.	
——		Wife of Loam Nearing.
Joseph,	1762, 1819, 57.	Married Charlotte Pettibone.
Uzziah.		Married Ruth Garrett.
Thomas,		Married —— Mallison.
Solon.		Married —— Olmsted.
Arabella.		Married Abraham Wilcox.
Alleluia,	1775.	Married 1st, Frederick Humphrey, Jun.; 2d, Ebenezer Miller.
Elisha,	1778.	Married Clarrissa Humphrey.

DANIEL DYER son of Benjamin and Margaret Dyer, married Sarah, daughter of Samuel and Anna Northway, and granddaughter of the noted Mrs. Sarah Woodford, who lived to be almost 101 years old. He commenced family state about 1774, and resided on the farm left by his honored father, Benjamin Dyer. Said premises are now owned by Luther Higley, Esq.

Parents.	Born. Died. Age.
Daniel Dyer,	1749, 1814, 65.
Sarah Northway,	1748, 1819, 70.

Children.	Born. Died. Age.	
Sarah,	1776.	Married Doct. Enoch Leavit.
Chloe,	1778.	Married Uriah Hopkins.
Candace,	1782.	Married Ashbel Moses,
Norman,	1786.	Married Diantha Roberts.
Zenas,	1788.	Married Sarah Chidsey.
Panthie,	1793.	Married 1st, Theophilus Dyer 2d, Fisk Beach.

They lost an infant in 1780.

DOCT. JOHN DYER, son of Benjamin Dyer Sen., lived and died single. He died 1793.

SOLOMON DILL. He removed from Groton to West Simsbury about the year 1753. He had one son and three daughters. He lived on the East Hill on the farm adjoining the Richard Case farm, and now known as the Morgan place; the house that is now standing, was built by him.

Parents.	Born. Died. Age.
Solomon Dill,	1731, 1800, 69.
Lydia Eggleston,	1727, 1789, 62.

Children.	Born. Died. Age.	
Eunice,	1753, 1815, 62.	Married Uriah Case.
Lois,	1759, 1812, 53.	Married Asa Case.
Lydia,	1764, 1813, 49.	Married Eber Humphrey.
Solomon, Jun.,	1767.	

DR. SOLOMON EVEREST was born April 11th, 1760, and died April 3d, 1822, aged 62 years. He married Miss Amelia Everett, of Winchester, about the year 1782, who was born, in 1767, and died October 22d, 1843, aged 86 years.

Dr. Everest, was a native of Salisbury, Conn., where he spent his youthful days. He studied the medical profession with Dr. Everett, of Winchester.

He first located, as a physician, in the town of Farmington, now Avon, about the year 1782. In 1796, he removed to West Simsbury, now Canton, where he resided the remainder of his life. As a citizen, of the town of Canton, he hardly had his rival. He was a member of the convention who formed the constitution of the state of Connecticut in 1818, several years judge of probate for the district of Simsbury, representative in the General Assembly of Connecticut, all of which civil appointments he discharged with ability, and the strictest integrity.

As a Christian, his character shone with uncommon luster. He was religious without enthusiasm, or austerity, a pillar of the church, wherein he was located. For twenty years, he officiated as deacon of the first Congregational church in Canton, was deeply studied in theology, strictly orthodox in the sentiments of the denomination to which he belonged. Being possessed of an ample fortune which he acquired by persevering industry, and having no lineal descendants to provide for, he was liberal in his lifetime, in aid of religious, and charitable purposes, and by will, left munificent bequests, for the same laudable objects.

As a physician and surgeon, he had but few equals, and educated a number of young men, who became eminent in their profession. The public, placed so much confidence in his professional skill, it was rare that further aid or counsel was solicited, even in extreme cases under his management. As a man, he left a distinguished mark, upon the age in which he lived, and his death, was considered an irreparable loss, to the town of Canton, and its vicinity.

The following incident, which occurred during his medical practice, to some may appear bordering on the ludicrous, but as it may serve to illustrate the happy expedients he could command, when necessary, is the apology for its insertion here.

On a certain occasion, he was called in great haste, to

attend to the case of a young girl, belonging to a somewhat marvelous, and eccentric family residing on the borders of a neighboring town, who was laboring under the dire malady of witchcraft. On repairing to the house where the scenes were enacting, he found the patient lying on a bed surrounded by her parents, and grandparents who were in the greatest consternation at what was passing before them, and who pathetically implored the doctor, if possible, to do something to alleviate the sufferings of the youthful patient. On inquiring into the symptoms, of the case, it appeared, the witches would torment her by violently pinching her arms and limbs, so that frequently, she would cry out in agony, the witches were pinching her, and on removing the clothing from her limbs, visible marks of violent pinches would appear on the flesh.

The doctor in the meantime, kept a sharp lookout, and came to the conclusion that the girl was the author of her troubles. For instance, when he was closely observing her, the witches would refrain from pinching, but if he chanced to leave the room, they would commence with renewed vigor.

Now for the remedy. He quietly remarked to the patient, that witchcraft was no uncommon complaint; that he had read and studied into the disorder. It was curable, and he could cure it. Two ways would accomplish the object; either burning or drowning the witches would be effective. He ordered a large cistern to be filled with water, and the sufferer, to be immersed in it, when the witches should again attack her. The operation was carried into effect; the first and second time, the witches became less and less frequent. Before the doctor left, he enjoined on the parents to continue the remedy, whenever the witches should make their appearance. On the doctors retiring, he remarked to his patient, if the water did not effect a cure, he had a large witch iron at home, he could bring, and by heating it red hot and appling it to the place affected he could burn the witches out of her, and fully accomplish a cure. She listened to his remarks with the most profound attention and eventually came to the conclusion, that the doctor's remedy, was worse than the disease.

On the succeeding day but one, anxious to learn the result of his prescriptions, he directed two of his students to make a casual call at the residence of the patient, and report progress.

It is needless to add, they returned with the joyful tidings, the patient was well, and peace and quiet was restored to the afflicted family.

——— EATON, with his wife, resided on a location between the family of Everest Case and sons, and Newell Miner. They left Canton about A. D. 1790, and went on to a farm in the north part of Burlington, where he spent the remainder of his life. But little is known to the writer respecting this family. Among his children were Samuel, Westover and Lorana; she connected in marriage with Levi Humphrey, son of Michael Humphrey, of Simsbury.

URIAH EDGECOMB, married Anna, daughter of Jacob Reed; was the first resident on the premises and erected the house which was for many years the residence of the late Elihu Olmsted and sons; the names of his children but little known. Among them were the wife of Josiah Russell, John, the wife of the late Erastus Daily, and Uriah, Jun. There may have been others. He died about A. D. 1810.

JOHN FOX was an early owner and resident in the house, and on the land now owned by the family of the late Robert Case, Jun., deceased, adjoining the Ward farm. It was understood in the early part of the life of the writer that he brought up the young man that bore the name of John F. Frazier, who married Deliverance, daughter of Josiah Clarke, who died in a time of distressing sickness in 1779. Very little is now known to the writer concerning that family.

HISTORICAL SKETCHES OF FOOTE GENEALOGY.

The compiler of the annexed statistics of the Foote family, is much indebted to Nathaniel Goodwin, Esq., in his excellent collection on Foote genealogy, published in Hartford, 1849.

NATHANIEL FOOTE (of whom Capt. John Foote, an early settler of West Simsbury, was a descendant of the fifth generation) was born in England, in 1593. At the age of twenty-two years he married Elizabeth Deming.

The precise year of his arrival in America is not definitely known. The first mention of his name occurs in the records of Massachusetts Bay, 1633, when he was admitted a freeman. In 1636, we find him a resident of Wethersfield. He had seven children, and died 1644, aged 51 years. His widow married Thomas Willis, a magistrate, and afterward governor of the colony, whom she survived. She died July 28th, 1683, aged 88 years.

SECOND GENERATION.

Children.

Elizabeth,	born about 1616, in England.
Nathaniel,	born about 1620, in England.
Mary,	born about 1623, in England.
Robert	born about 1627, in England.
Francis,	born about 1629, in England.
Sarah,	born about 1632, in England.
Rebecca,	born about 1634, in America.

NATHANIEL FOOTE, of Wethersfield, married Elizabeth ——, 1640, and died 1655, aged 34 years.

THIRD GENERATION.

Children.

Nathaniel,	born January 10, 1647.
Samuel,	born May 1, 1649.
Daniel,	born May 1, 1652.
Elizabeth,	born May 1, 1654.

SAMUEL FOOTE, of Hatfield, was married to Mary Merrick, of Springfield, in the same State, 1671. He died September 7th, 1689, aged 40 years. His widow, Mary Foote, died October 3d, 1690.

FOURTH GENERATION.

Children.

Nathaniel,	born	1672.	
Mary,	born July	9, 1674.	She died in childhood.
Samuel,	born		Slain by the Indians at Deerfield, February 29th, 1704.
Mary,	born February,	28, 1680.	
Sarah,	born February,	26, 1682.	
Eleazor,	born September,	5, 1684.	
Thomas,	born November,	24, 1686.	
Daniel	born February,	6, 1689.	Killed by falling from a load of hay.

DANIEL FOOTE. first of Hartford, was married to Mary Collyer, November 19th, 1718. He removed to Duncaster, Simsbury, where he purchased an extensive farm and resided on it the remainder of his life.

While descending from a load of hay he fell to the ground forward of the wheels; the cattle took fright, went forward, the wheels passing over him, caused his death about one hour thereafter, July 15th, 1740. His widow, Mrs. Mary Foote, died June, 1769. aged 71. She died at the residence of her son, Capt John Foote, in West Simsbury, and was interred in the North burying-ground.

FIFTH GENERATION.

Children.

Samuel,	born October	4, 1719, in Hartford.
Mary,	born November	20, 1721, in Simsbury.
Daniel, the pioneer,	born April	27, 1724, in Simsbury.
Joseph,	born February	17, 1727, in Simsbury.

John,	born	1729.	
Rachel,	born	1731.	Died January 21st, 1737.
Sarah,	born	1732.	
Rachel,	born March,	1736.	

CAPT. JOHN FOOTE. He removed from Duncaster, in the old parish, about the year 1753. He was twice married; first to Rosanna Humphrey, daughter of Jonathan Humphrey, of the same town, in 1753. Mrs. Rosanna Foote died October 10th, 1793, aged 62 years. His second wife was Mary Fowler, of Salem, and she survived him. He resided on the farm now owned and occupied by William E. Brown, near the intersection of the roads, and about twenty-five rods south-west of the present house.

Capt. John Foote died Sept. 15th, 1812, aged 82 years He had children only by his first wife.

SIXTH GENERATION.

Children.

Rosanna,	born October	14, 1754.	Married Ephraim Mills; died October 23d, 1814, aged 62.
John, Jun.,	born January	9, 1760.	Married Lois Mills, died June 13th, 1803, aged 42.
Luther,	born March	5, 1761.	Married 1st, Temperance Hays; 2d, Anna Bronson; died March 5th, 1834, aged 74.
Lucretia,	born October	28, 1763.	Married 1st, Elias Case; 2d, Dudley Case; died October 1st, 1844, aged 80.
Rachel,	born November	27, 1766.	Married Dan Case; died August, 1784, aged 18.
Hilpah Rosiette,	born October	18, 1772.	Married Lawton Marcy; died March, 1846, aged 78.

Number of children seven. Capt. John Foote was a man of robust constitution, an incessant laborer and farmer through life.

JOHN FOOTE, JUN., was married to Lois, daughter of Dea. Benjamin Mills, of that part of the ancient town of New Hartford, now forming part of the town of Canton. He settled, and remained through life, on the farm now owned and occupied by his son, Dea. Lancel Foote.

Parents.	Born. Died. Age.	
John Foote, Jun.,	1760, 1803, 42.	Died suddenly.
Lois Mills,	1762, 1802, 39.	

Children.	Born. Died. Age.	
An infant.		
Clara,	1784, 1789, 6.	
Laura,	1786, 1855, 69.	Married Louis M. Norton, of Goshen.
Miles,	1788.	Married Clarinda Barber.
Lancel,	1790.	Married Laura Humphrey.
Hershel,	1793.	Married Pamela B. Townsend, of Albany.
Clara,	1795, 1837, 42.	Married Luke Barber.
Stiles,	1797, 1798.	
Stella,	1799, 1839, 40.	Married Chester Wadsworth, of Becket, Mass.
John Stiles,	1803.	Married Margaret Todd, of Pennsylvania.

ANCESTRY OF THE FRANCIS GARRETT FAMILY.

SAMUEL TULLER married Sarah, daughter of John Mills, about the year 1715; they had three sons, viz., Samuel, Joseph and Isaac, the latter born fatherless. The widow afterward married Francis Garrett, a Frenchman, by whom she had five children.

Children.	Born. Died. Age.	
Sarah,	1723, 1821, 98.	Married Oliver Humphrey.
Susannah,	1725, 1805, 80.	Married William Woodford.
John,	1727.	
Francis,	1729.	Married Ruth, daughter of Capt. James Case.
Anna,	1731.	Married 1st, James Northway; 2d, John Phelps,

The first Francis Garrett, died 1731, and his widow married Capt. Joseph Woodford, with whom she lived the remainder of his life. After his death in 1744, she spent the remainder of her days with Mr. William Woodford, son of Capt. Joseph Woodford, who married her daughter Susannah, in 1745. She lived until 1797, and died in her 101st year. Maj. John Garrett, her son, removed to Wyoming, in Pennsylvania, where he was killed in a battle with the Indians. His widow with other women and children, escaped the death by which the men had fallen, by fleeing (as they were instructed) to a raft that lay in the Susquehannah river, and floating down the stream, but their property was all destroyed that could be, by the Indians.

FRANCIS GARRETT, 2D, with his wife, Ruth Case, daughter of Capt. James Case, and sister of Capt. Josiah Case, settled in West Simsbury, in 1746, on lands at the confluence of the Albany and Litchfield turnpike, west of the William Stone buildings. He was a blacksmith by trade. He died of consumption. His widow was married to Gideon Case.

Parents.	Born. Died. Age.
Francis Garret,	1729.
Ruth Case.	

Children.	Born. Died. Age.	
Rufus, 1st,	1754, 1760, 6.	
Ruth,	1756.	Married Uzziah Dyer.
Francis,	1759.	

Rufus, 2d,	1762, 1831, 69.	Married 1st, Chloe Hills; 2d, Mary Tuller; 3d, Charlotte Moses.
Thias,	1764, 1838, 74.	Married Miriam Case, daughter of Isaac Case; died 1847, aged 77.
James,	1767.	Married Apphia Hill; died 1839, aged 75.
Theodore,	1769.	
Ruth, 2d,	1772.	Married Thomas Dyer, Jun.

DR. ELISHA GRAHAM. He came from Wintonbury, now Bloomfield, with his wife, Anna Humphrey, daughter of Thomas Humphrey, 2d, to West Simsbury in the year 1753, and settled on the farm now owned and occupied by Watson Case, 1st. There were six children in this family.

Parents.	Born. Died. Age.	
Elisha Graham,	1734, 1805, 72.	
Anna Humphrey,	1734, 1793, 59.	Daughter of Thomas Humphrey, 2d.

Children.	Born. Died. Age.	
Elisha,	1753.	Married Hannah Merritt.
William,	1756.	Married Saphira Owen.
Augustus.		
Freeman,*	1762, 1819, 55.	Married 1st, Lydia Phelps: 2d, Lydia May.
Infant,	1766, 1766.	
Anna,	1769, 1827, 58.	Married Ashbel Graham.

ISAAC GRAHAM, a brother of Elisha settled on what is called the Cook farm, on Bald Hill, about the year 1752.

---

*Freeman Graham occasioned his own death by stabbing himself with a butcher knife, August 1st, 1817, and died August 2d.

Parents.	Born. Died. Age.	
Isaac Graham,	1728, 1807, 79.	
Sarah Moses.		

Children.	Born. Died. Age.	
Isaac, Jun.		
Sarah.		Married Thomas Caverlee.
George.		
Ardelice.		Married Seba Moses.
Timothy, 1st,	1768, 1775, 7.	
Lucy,		Married Thomas Sanford, Jun.
Candace.		
Timothy, 2d.		Married Ruth Wilcox.
Annis,		Married Elijah Arnold.

DANIEL GRAHAM, a brother to Isaac and Elisha, with his first wife, Zerviah Moses, came and settled on the place now (1855) owned by Chester Case, about the year 1756.

Parents.	Born. Died. Age.
Daniel Graham,	1736, 1827, 91.
1st wife, Zerviah Moses,	1740, 1763, 23.
2d wife, Lois Phelps,	1747, 1776, 29.
3d wife, Anna Roberts.	1748, 1821, 73.

Children.	Born. Died. Age.	
Daniel, Jun.,	1759, 1808, 49.	Married.
Lois,	1764.	Married Michael Segar.
Israel,	1767, 1813, 46.	Married Roxana Case.
Ashbel,	1768, 1813, 45.	Married Anna Graham.
Jemmy.		Married Unice Gains.
Zerviah,	1775,	Married Amos Edgerton,
Erastus,	1844.	Married Hilpah Roby.

MOSES GAINES, with his wife Lucy, daughter of Thomas and Elizabeth Barber, commenced their family state about A. D. 1762. They resided on the farm now owned by Henry Barber, till about A. D. 1775. Mr. John Barber, Jun., then became the owner of that farm, and Mr. Gaines rented the farm of Ephraim Buell's heirs, till 1784, when he went to the north part of New Hartford, on the east river, where he spent the remainder of his days.

Parents.	Born. Died. Age.	
Moses Gaines,*	1731, 1817, 86.	
Lucy Barber,	1742, 1831, 89.	

Children.	Born. Died. Age.	
Moses, Jun.,	1764,	Married Hannah Miller.
Lucy,	1762, 1849, 87.	Married Elijah Simons.
Lois,	1766.	Married 1st, James Simons, 2d, —— Loomis.
Unice,	1769.	Married 1st, Jemmy Graham; 2d, Daniel Pettibone.
Elizabeth,	1772.	Married Levi Hart.
Alpheus,	1774, 1845, 71.	Married Susan Miller.
Enoch,	1777.	Married Anna Warner.
Theresse,	1779.	Married Richard Case, 5th.
Ruth,	1781.	Married Jehiel Wilcox.

PHILIP HARRIS, with his wife Rhoda, resided on the premises now owned by Lucian Bidwell, and was its first owner. They were the parents of the wife of Asher Hinman, whose given name was Mary, and also the wife of the late Capt. Amaziah Humphrey, of Simsbury. Their farm became the property of Asher Hinman and wife and from them passed into the hands of Thomas Bidwell, Jun.

JOHN HILL, Jun., son of John Hill, Sen., with his first wife, Isabel Alford, settled in 1740, in the East Hill school district. They resided on the farm now owned by Nelson Aldridge. They had by the first marriage one son and two

* Of this family, Moses, Jun., and his wife, also Eunice, Elizabeth and Enoch, are still living.

daughters; the daughters were married to two men by the name of Covey, of the religious order of the Seventh Day Baptists; they settled in Burlington. For second wife he married Isabel, a daughter of Thomas Eggleston. They had six more children.

Parents.	Born.	Died.	Age.	
John Hill, Jun.,	1725,	1795,	70.	
1st wife, Isabel Alford.				Daughter of Nathaniel Alford, Sen.
2d wife, Isabel Eggleston,	1733,	1818,	85.	

Children by 1st wife.	Born.	Died.	Age.	
John, 3d,				Married Mary Case.
Daughter.				Married Mr. Covey.
Daughter.				Married Mr. Covey.

Children by 2d wife.	Born.	Died.	Age.	
Jedadiah.				Married Miss Kilby.
Elijah.				Married Esther Tuller.
Chloe,		1794.		Married Rufus Garrett.
Welthy,	1767.	1852,	85.	Married Jabez O. Gleason.
Keziah,		1827,	57.	Married Thaddeus Tuller.
Anna,		1819.		Married Nahum Barber.

DARIUS HILL, son of John Hill, Sen., and half brother of John Hill, Jun. He married Lois, daughter of Benoni Moses. They resided on the East Hill, on the premises, which after his death were owned and occupied by the late Titus Case, deceased. They had four sons and three daughters. The sons all died in early life; the three youngest, with one grandchild died in the beginning of the winter 1798–9, together with the father, in the short time of little more than one month; all of dysentery.

Parents.	Born.	Died.	Age.
Darius Hill,	1749,	1799,	50.
Lois Moses,		1749.	

Children.	Born. Died. Age.	
Lois, about	1770.	Married Theodore Shelden.
Darius, Jun.,	1772, 1788, 16.	Died of Consumption,
Sarah.		Married Frederick Sheldon.
Arden,	1776, 1799, 23.	Died in the western army; drowned by failing through the ice.
Rachel.		
Elias,	1798.	
Asa,	1798.	

The mother and her three daughters, left the town near the beginning of the present century, and but little is now known respecting the family.

ASHER HINMAN, with his wife Mary, daughter of Philip Harris, resided on the farm now owned by Lucian Bidwell, in the fore part of their family state till about the year 1786. They then removed to the west side of the river, where they lived the remainder of their lives.

Parents.	Born. Died. Age.
Asher Hinman,	1741, 1809, 68.
Mary Harris,	1821.

Children.	Born. Died. Age.	
Eliza.		Married Uriah Beach.
Amasa,	1768,	Married Polly Hinman.
Zerah,	1771, 1848, 78.	Married Anna Mills, daughter of Moses Mills.
Rhoda.		Married Moses Mills, Jun.
Philip Harris.		
Cretia.		Married Elias Mills.
Arad.		Married Polly Richards.
Asher,	1852.	Married Eunice Alderman.

OLIVER HUMPHREY, Esq., the first magistrate in West Simsbury, was son of Jonathan Humphrey, who was born in 1688. Jonathan Humphrey was son of the first Samuel. Oliver Humphrey, Esq., was brother to Jonathan and Solomon. He removed to West Simsbury about 1742, and resided on the premises lately owned by William Stone, Esq., Suffrage Village. He had eleven children who lived to adult years, four sons and seven daughters, eight of whom connected in life and had children. The family were considered as conspicuous members in the community.

Parents.	Born.	Died.	Age.
Oliver Humphrey,	1720,	1792,	72.
Sarah Garret,	1723,	1821,	98.

Children.	Born.	Died.	Age.	
Sarah,	1744,	1795,	59.	Married 1st, Abraham Case, Jr., Rev. Abraham Fowler.
Lois,	1746,	1800,	64.	Married Bildad Barber.
Ruth,	1748,	1822,	74.	Married Gideon Mills, Jr.
Oliver, Jun.,	1750.	1776,	26.	Died in the army.
Erastus,	1752,	1776,	24.	Died in the army.
Reuben,	1754,	1830,	76.	Married Anna Humphrey.
Rachel,	1756,	1831,	75.	Married George Humphrey.
Asher,	1758,	1826,	68.	Married Chloe Humphrey.
Mercy,	1761,	1826,	65.	Married Rev. Jeremiah Hallock.
Esther,	1763,	1808,	45.	Married Eber Alford.
Lavinia,	1765,	1848,	83.	Married Thomas Bidwell, Jun

MAJ. REUBEN HUMPHREY, third son of Oliver Humphrey, Esq., married Anna, daughter of Capt. Ezekiel Humphrey. He resided on the premises and erected the dwelling-house at the junction of the roads west of the William Stone place. The house is now owned by——————. He was a man of fine native talents, and useful attainments, such as go to make up a useful citizen. He was early in life appointed to the office of justice of the peace, and also filled various posts of high responsibility and honor, both in his native, and adopted state. He sustained the rank of major in the militia, and was keeper of the Newgate prison for five years. He, in 1802, removed to Onondaga county in the State of New York, where he shared largely in the confidence of his fellow-citizens.

Parents.	Born.	Died.	Age.
Reuben Humphrey,	1754,	1830,	76.
Anna Humphrey,	1758,	1826,	68.

Children.	Born.	Died.	Age.
Guy.	1807,	1807.	
Reuben, Jun.			
Gad.			

CAPT. ASHER HUMPHREY, fourth son of Oliver Humphrey, Esq., married Chloe, daughter of Capt. Ezekiel Humphrey. He resided on the premises, and erected the dwelling-house now owned by Pomeroy Higley.

Parents.	Born.	Died.	Age.
Asher Humphrey,	1758,	1826,	68.
Chloe Humphrey,	1762,	1813,	51.

Children.	Born.	Died.	Age.	
Oliver.				Married Rhoda Woodford.
Erastus.				Married Anna London.
Sophia.				
Julius.				
Norris.				
Mary.				
Emily.				
John.				
Trueman.				

SOLOMON HUMPHREY, Sen. He was brother of Jonathan and Oliver, and removed from the old parish to West Simsbury, about the year 1742. He settled on the premises now occupied by Everest Case and sons, and little to the south-east of the present house.

Parents.	Born.	Died.	Age.
Solomon Humphrey,	1722,	1798,	76.
Naomi Higley,	1726,	1817,	91.

Children.	Born.	Died.	Age.	
Naomi,	1749,	1816,	69.	Married Andrew Mills.
Solomon,	1747,	1751,	4.	Died in youth.
Ruggles,	1751,	1802,	51.	Married Lucy Case.
Solomon,	1752,	1834,	81.	Father of Rev. Heman Humphrey, late president of Amherst College. Married 1st, Lucy Case, daughter of Ezekiel Case; 2d, Hannah Brown.
Esther,	1758,	1812,	52.	
Augustus,	1771.			Married daughter of Ephraim Barber; now living, 1856.

THE ANCESTRY OF OLIVER AND SOLOMON HUMPHREY.

MICHAEL HUMPHREY,* of Windsor, was the ancestor of the Humphreys in this region. He married Priscilla Grant, in the year 1647. Their children were John, born 1650; Mary, born 1652; Samuel, born 1656; Martha, born 1663; Sarah, born 1658; Abigail, born 1665; Hannah, born 1669.

Lieut. SAMUEL HUMPHREY, son of Michael and Priscilla Humphrey, was born 1656, and died 1736. Their

* His descendants, are scattered through the Northern and Western States.

children were Samuel, Jonathan, Charles, Noah, Mary, Elizabeth and Abigail.

The first Jonathan Humphrey, son of Lieut. Samuel Humphrey, married Mercy Ruggles, daughter of the Rev. Mr. Ruggles, of Suffield. Their children were Jonathan, Mercy, married Dea. Michael Humphrey, Oliver, Solomon, Esther, who married John Owen, Apphia, married John Higley, and Rosanna, married John Foot.

RUGGLES HUMPHREY, son of Solomon Humphrey, Sen. He received his given name probably to honor and perpetuate the name of his grandmother, Mercy, the daughter of the Rev. Mr. Ruggles, of Suffield. He married Lucy the daughter of Amos Case, Sen. They had no children. He resided on the premises now owned by Roswell Barnes, lying in the East Hill school-district. He gave part of the farm he left, to the Connecticut Missionary Society. He was born 1751; died 1802, aged 51. His wife Lucy, born 1752, died 1837, aged 85.

SOLOMON HUMPHREY, Jun., son of Solomon and Naomi Humphrey, married for his first wife, Lucy, daughter of Ezekiel and Lucy Case, A. D. 1772, and for his second wife Hannah, daughter of Capt. John and Mrs. Hannah Brown, married 1778.

He resided the first twelve years of his family state with his father on the place now owned by Levi, 2d, and Orestus Case, in the East Hill school-district near the confines of Simsbury, until the year 1785. He then removed to Burlington, and there resided until 1813, and then removed to Barkhampstead where he resided the remainder of his life. He had two children by his first wife, and thirteen by his second.

Parents.	Born.	Died.	Age.
Solomon Humphrey,	1752,	1834.	81.
1st wife, Lucy Case,	1754,	1776,	22.

	Born. Died. Age.	
2d wife, Hannah Brown,	1758. 1825, 66.	

Children.	Born. Died. Age.	
Horace,	1772, 1855, 82.	
Solomon, Jun.,	1774, 1830, 56.	
Heman,	1779.	Late president of Amherst College; married Sophia, daughter of Dea. Noah Porter, of Farmington.
Lucy,	1781, 1809, 28.	Jason Squires' 2d wife.
Luther,	1783,	Married 1st, Sarah H. Lawton; 2d, widow Julia B. Treat.
Infant,	1784, 1784.	
Infant,	1786, 1786.	
Infant,	1787, 1788.	
Clarinda,	1789.	Married Harvey Webster.
Infant,	1791, 1791.	
Candace,	1792.	
Naomi,	1794.	Married Henry Barber.
Hannah,	1796,	Married Alson Barber.
Electa,	1799.	Married Sidney Hart.
Harriet,	1802.	

CAPT. EZEKIEL HUMPHREY, SEN., son of Samuel Humphrey, 2d. Capt. Ezekiel, was grandson of the first Samuel Humphrey in the line of Samuel Humphrey. He removed from the old parish to West Simsbury in 1743, and settled on the parsonage lot now owned by Dr. B. A. Kasson. He had ten children, five sons and five daughters, all of whom married and had children, except Lydia.

Parents.	Born. Died. Age.
Ezekiel Humphrey,	1720, 1795, 75.
Elizabeth Pettibone,	1724, 1792, 68.

Children.	Born. Died. Age.	
Ezekiel,	1746, 1802, 56.	Married —— Scott.
Elijah,	1748, 1788, 40.	Married Chloe Wilcox.

Elizabeth,	1750, 1808, 58.	Married 1st Daniel Case, Jun.; 2d, Elisha Case.
Frederick,	1753, 1821, 68.	Married Ruth Teller.
George,	1756, 1813, 57.	Married 1st, Elizabeth Pettibone; 2d. Rachel Humphrey.
Anna,	1758, 1826, 68.	Married Reuben Humphrey.
Giles,	1760, 1816, 56.	Married Elizabeth, daughter of Dea. Abraham Case.
Chloe,	1762, 1813, 51.	Married Asher Humphrey.
Betsy,	1767.	Married Sylvanus Humphrey,
Lydia,	1769.	Married 1st. Alexander Pettibone; 2d, Samuel Webster.

CAPT. EZEKIEL HUMPHREY, JUN., with his wife, ——— Scott, settled in family state about ———. He was a sea-captain, and of course was absent from his native town a great part of the prime of life. They had two sons and one daughter. He died in 1802, aged 56.

CAPT. ELIJAH HUMPHREY, son of Capt. Ezekiel Humphrey, Sen., and Brother to Capt. Ezekiel Humphrey, Jun. He was also a sea-captain. He married Chloe, daughter of Ephraim Wilcox. They had one son Allen, who in ——— removed from this town; one daughter, Chloe, died of scarlet fever in 1793, aged eleven years, and one son died in 1778, aged five years, and a double monument was erected to their memory in the South burying-ground, by their older brother Allen at the age of twenty-four years. The father was lost at sea in the year 1788, aged forty-two. The widow afterward married James Olcott.

Capt. FREDERICK HUMPHREY, son of Capt. Ezekiel Humphrey and of the fourth degree in descent from the first Michael Humphrey, of Windsor. He married Ruth Tuller, daughter of Ensign Isaac Tuller. He resided in the early part of his family state, in the north-west part of Avon, then called Whortlebury Hill, until 1789, when he built the most ancient house now standing in Collinsville, where he resided the remainder of his life. For many of the last years of his life, he was the owner of about four-fifths of the land on both sides of the river where the village of Collinsville is now situated.

He was a man of stately and robust frame, with strength and resolution in proportion to it. In the year 1792, he, in company with his brother, Col. George Humphrey, erected a forge for the manufacture of iron. It was situated on the then east branch of the river, at or very near the site of the old stone shop that has a steeple and bell. It was so much damaged by the Jefferson flood, so called, in 1801, that it went into decay from about that time, and was swept off by the great flood of 1804. A grist-mill and saw-mill were afterward erected there, but were both removed in 1827, or soon after, to make room for the manufacturing establishment of the Collins Co.

Parents.	Born.	Died.	Age.
Frederick Humphrey,	1753,	1821,	68.
Ruth Teller,	1755,	1818,	63.

Children.	Born.	Died.	Age.	
Frederick, Jun.,	1775,	1830,	55.	Married Alla Dyer.
Isaac,	1777,	1856,	79.	Married Miss Boughton.
Alexander,	1778,	1850,	72.	Married Roxy R. Brown; died 1855.
Ruth,	1783.			Married Luke Hayden.
Rufus,	1785.			Married Lucinda Woodford.
Sylvester,	1786.			Married Phebe Bidwell.
Zada,	1790,	1818,	28.	Elias Woodford's first wife.
Romanta,	1788.			Married Huldah Woodford.
Fanny,	1793.			Elias Woodford's second wife.
Correl,	1795,	1835,	40.	Married Almira Humphrey.

Col. GEORGE HUMPHREY, a son of Capt. Ezekiel and Elizabeth Humphrey. His ancestry, from the first settlers in Windsor, was as follows, viz.: first Michael, second Samuel 1st, third Samuel 2d, fourth Ezekiel 1st. He was a prominent and worthy citizen in the various departments of public and private life. He bore a part in the Revolutionary war in early life. He possessed to a good degree the confidence of his fellow-citizens. He honorably filled various offices in the military department in the prime of life. At the time of his decease he was in the capacity of justice of the peace, judge of probate, and member of the state legislature. He resided on the parsonage farm left by his father. He was connected with his brother Frederick, in the building and ownership of the forge which was built in 1792.

He married for his first wife, Elizabeth, daughter of Capt. Abraham Pettibone, and granddaughter of Samuel Pettibone, Jun. For his second wife, he married Rachel, daughter of Oliver Humphrey, Esq.

Parents.	Born.	Died.	Age.
George Humphrey,	1756,	1813,	57.
Elizabeth Pettibone,	1756,	1784,	28.
Rachel Humphrey,	1756,	1831,	75,

Children.	Born.	Died.	Age.	
Clarissa	1778,	1779,	1.	
Clarissa,	1780.			Married Elisha Dyer.
George, Jun.,	1782,	1836,	54.	Married 1st, Candace Case; 2d, Lois Woodford.
Jerusha,	1783,	1784,	1.	
Elizabeth,	1785.			Married 1st, Dudley Humphrey.
Cornelia,	1787.			Married Abraham Griswold.
Decius,	1789.			Married Laura Adams.
Stelly,	1790,	1846,	56.	Married 1st, Lester Cone.
Emily,	1792.			Married Ralph Meecham.
Laura,	1795.			Married Lancel Foote.
Hector,	1797.			President of the college at Annapolis, Maryland.

SAMUEL HUMPHREY, the third of the name of Samuel. He married Mary Wilcox, in 1734, a twin to Nathaniel Wilcox. He removed from the Old Parish to West Simsbury about the year 1741. He was born in 1710; supposed to have died about 1760; aged about fifty years. Mary his wife, was born 1719; died 1756, aged 37. He resided on or near the site now occupied by Pomeroy Higley. They had six children, three sons, and three daughters, who all lived to connect in life, and have children; whether any died in early life is not known.

Children.	Born. Died. Age.	
Samuel,	1734, 1804, 70.	Married Prudence Mills.
Azubah,	1737, 1816, 79.	Married Thomas Dyer.
Hannah,	1740, 1821, 81.	Married Benjamin Mills.
William,	1742, 1773, 31.	Married Hepzibah Merrell.
Theophilus,	1744, 1826, 82.	Married Hepzibah Cornish.
Mary,	1746, 1830, 84.	Married Daniel Morgan, grandfather of the present Daniel Morgan.

WILLIAM HUMPHREY, the second son of Samuel Humphrey, 3d, married Hepzibah Merrell, A. D., 1762. They resided in that part of New Hartford that is now Canton, on the place now occupied by John and Mark Pike.

Parents.	Born. Died. Age.	
William Humphrey,		Married 1762.
Hepzibah Merrell,	1817.	Married 2d, Sylvanus Case.

Children.	Born. Died. Age.	
William, Jun.,	1763.	Married Elizabeth Roberts.
Roswell,	1765.	Married Betsey or Elizabeth Seymour.
Susannah,	1768.	Married George Wilcox.
Arnold P.,	1770, 1851, 80.	Married 1st, Amelia Spencer; 2d, Rosanna Mills.

SAMUEL HUMPHREY, commonly called Master Sam, the fourth of the name and fifth degree (inclusive) from the first Michael. He married Prudence, daughter of John Mills, about A. D. 1759. He resided on the place, and in the house now occupied by his youngest son, Eber. He was lame, taught school, and wrote much.

Parents.	Born.	Died.	Age.	
Samuel Humphrey,	1734,	1804,	70.	Son of Samuel Humphrey, 3d.
Prudence Mills,	1734,	1805,	71.	

Children.	Born.	Died.	Age.	
Samuel, Jun., the fifth,				Married Zerviah Wilcox.
Phebe,	1763,	1848,	85.	Married Abisha Forbes.
Lemuel G. Gordon.				Married Dorcas Case.
Rosetta.				Married John Mark.
Dorthy or Dolly.				Married David Cooper.
Ichabod.				Married Esther Olmsted.
Mary.				Married Oliver Brewster, State of New York.
Eber.	1776.			Married 1st, Lydia Dill; 2d, Ruth Rising.

JONATHAN HUMPHREY, a descendant of the first Jonathan Humphrey, of Simsbury. He resided in the East Hill, school-district, on land situated between the school-house, and the farm belonging to Calvin Case, Jun. It fell to the late Cyrus Humphrey. He had seven children four by his first wife, and three by his second wife, who died in 1794.

Parents.	Born.	Died.	Age.
Jonathan Humphrey.		1796.	

Children by 1st wife.	Born.	Died.	Age.	
Lucina.				
Cyrus,		1822.		Married Amy Baldwin, of Waterbury.
Aurelia.				
Amoret.				Died unmarried.

Children by 2d wife.	Born. Died. Age.	
Jonathan, Jun.,	1830.	Married widow of Jonathan Andruss, Jr.
Ruth,	1789, 1829, 40.	First wife of Plinny Griswold.
Alma.		Married Barzilla Roberts.

LIEUT. CHARLES HUMPHREY, 2D, a son of Charles Humphrey, with his wife Sarah, daughter of Benajah Humphrey, settled in West Simsbury, about the year 1753. Their first buildings were erected on the east end of the farm. He afterward built and lived on the western part of his farm at the site now occupied by his grandson, Charles Humphrey and Bera Case. The young man now living on the East Hill and on the old site, bearing the name of Charles, is of the fifth generation from the first Charles; the name of Charles, being used five generations in succession.

The wife of Lieut. Charles had four husbands: 1st, Charles Humphrey, 2d, Seth Smith, 3d Elisha Graham, 4th Amasa Case.

Parents.	Born. Died. Age.
Charles Humphrey,	1734, 1779, 45.
Sarah Humphrey,	1736, 1823, 87.

Children.	Born. Died, Age.	
Charles, Jun.,	1754, 1805, 51.	Married Hannah Case.
Mary,	1756.	Married Phineas Noble.
Benajah,	1759, 1803, 44.	Married Thede Case.

CHARLES HUMPHREY, 3D, a son of Lieut. Charles Humphrey, and great grandson of Lieut. Samuel Humphrey. He resided on the East Hill by his father, Charles Humphrey, 2d.

Parents.	Born. Died. Age.	
Charles Humphrey,	1754, 1805, 51.	
Hannah Case,	1754, 1808, 54.	Daughter of Dea. Abraham Case.

Children.	Born. Died. Age.	
Mary, or Polly,	1782, 1822, 40.	Married Ira Case.
Charles, 4th,	1785.	Married Laura Case; died 1842, aged 54.
Rachel,	1790.	Married Abel Case, 2d.

DEA. THEOPHILUS HUMPHREY, son of Samuel Humphrey, 3d. He with his wife, removed to West Simsbury about the year 1764, and settled at the south-east part of the town. He afterward lived in the Old Parish a few years, and in 1782, he again removed to West Simsbury, and settled on the premises now owned by his grandson, Loin H. Humphrey, in the Center district.

Parents.	Born. Died. Age.	
Theophilus Humphrey,	1744, 1826, 82.	
1st wife, Hepzibah, Cornish,	1742, 1800, 58.	Daughter of Elisha Cornish.
2d wife, Diana Averit,	1752, 1843, 91.	

Children.	Born. Died. Age.	
James,	1765, 1830, 65.	Married 1st, Keturah Case; 2d, Diadama Garret.
Hepzibah,	1767.	Married Jesse Barber.
Alvin,	1769, 1847, 77.	Married 1st, Almira Case; 2d, Mary Hays.
Child.		Died in infancy.
Amelia,	1774, 1808, 34.	Married Jonathan Barber, 2d.
Theophilus, Jun.,	1776, 1851, 75.	Married 1st, Cynthia Hayden; 2d Miss Cornish.
Loin,	1777, 1854, 77.	Married Rhoda Case.
Plinny,	1780, 1852, 72.	Married Rhoda Higley, daughter of Seth Higley.

Thede,	1782.	Married Thomas Sugden, Jun.
Dudley,	1784, 1826, 42.	Married Elizabeth Humphrey.
Keziah,	1786, 1818, 32.	Married Stephen H. Atwater.

Rev. JEREMIAH HALLOCK was born at Brookhaven, Long Island, 1758. At the age of eight years, he with his parents removed to Goshen, Mass. Mr. Hallock was licensed to preach the gospel in 1784, and was ordained over the church and society of West Simsbury, (now Canton,) in 1785. He was honored for his faithful and unwearied efforts in the service of his divine Lord and Master; during the entire term of his ministry, extending over a period of forty years, and terminating with his life, he exerted a rare influence, not only over the people of his charge, but throughout an extensive circle of acquaintance. His memory is yet venerated. He died June, 1826, aged 68. He married Mercy Humphrey, daughter of Oliver Humphrey, Esq., in 1786. She was born in 1762; died 1826, aged 64 years.

Their first son, Jeremiah Humphrey Hallock, was born 1790; graduated at Williams College, Mass., 1809, and entered the profession of law. He was long the presiding judge in the Ohio Circuit Court, and died at Steubenville, Ohio, 1848, at the age of 58.

The second son, William Homan Hallock, was born 1795; yet survives, and owns and occupies the place occupied by his father, excepting the dwelling-house, which is now owned and occupied by Mr. Hallock's successor in the ministry, Rev. Jairus Burt.

Daughter Sarah was born 1799: died. 1813, aged 14 years.

ITEMS OF HISTORY OF THE HIGLEY FAMILY, AND RACE OF DESCENDANTS.

JOHN HIGLEY, Esq., was among the early settlers in Windsor, and among the early settlers in Simsbury. The place where he and his numerous descendants lived in Simsbury, was north-west from Tariffville. It was formerly called Higley town, after the name of its inhabitants. He married Hannah, daughter of John and Hannah Drake, and granddaughter of Dea. John and Hannah Moore, married, A. D. 1671. He was honored with many of the highest offices in the gift of his fellow-citizens, being the first appointed justice of the peace, and soon after, judge of the county court. He represented the town at the General Assembly, for many sessions, subsequent to the year 1698. He was the first military captain, being chosen in 1698, an office at that time of great dignity. His children were John Jun., or 2d, born 1673; Jonathan, born 1675; Hannah, born 1677; Rebecca, born 1679; Brewster, born 1681. Of these, Hannah, the oldest daughter, married Joseph Trumbull, in 1704, and became the mother of the first Governor Jonathan Trumbull, and his honorable descendants, who for many years held a high rank among Connecticut worthies.

Brewster, the third son, was married A. D. 1708, to Esther, (or Hester,) daughter of Nathaniel Holcomb, and granddaughter of the first Thomas Holcomb. Their children were Brewster, Jun., born 1711; Joseph, born 1713; David, born 1715; Hannah, born 1717; Hester, born 1719; John, (the third of the name,) born 1721; Elizabeth, born 1723; Naomi, born 1725. These eight persons, who are all that are known of as belonging to this family, lived to great age; their several ages when added together make the round number of 646 years, which divided by eight, makes the average longevity to be about eighty years and nine months. There are now living in Canton several families, who, through the female line are descendants of this ancient Higley family. Hannah, the oldest daughter, became the wife of Elijah Owen, the first, about the year 1734. She had by him, Rebecca, who married Benedict Alford, and removed to Vermont. She lived to the age of 95 years. One child died in infancy; Elijah Jun., or 2d, who died at Otis, in 1814, aged 76; Hannah, was the wife of Capt. John Brown, and the mother of the Brown family in Canton, and died there in the year 1831, aged 91 years. The aforementioned Hannah Higley, widow of Elijah Owen, for a second mariage, married Peletiah Mills, Esq., in the year 1748. Their children were Peletiah, Samuel, Roger, Martha, Eli, Frederick, Susanna and Elihu, the father of the Mills in the town of Bloomfield. Martha married a Barnard; Susanna married a Hubbard; Hester married Capt. Josiah Case, and was the mother of the late Capt. Fithen Case, and that connection; Elizabeth married Rev. Gideon Mills, minister of West Simsbury; Naomi married Solomon Humphrey, Sen., or 1st, and was the mother of Solomon Humphrey, Jun., or 2d, and that connection. Brewster, Jun., the oldest son, was the father of the wife of Abel Case, Sen., and that connection, also grand parent of the wife of the late Plinny Humphrey, and the mother of Norman Case. John, the fourth son of Brewster, Sen., and the third of the name of John, married Apphia, daughter of Jonathan Humphrey, the first, and great granddaughter of the first Michael Humphrey. He resided a part of his family state in Canton, though mostly in Old Simsbury. His sons were John, Carmi, Obed, Isaac, Eber, Roger, and Job. His daughters were the wife of Dea. Jared Mills, and the wife of Job Mills. John, Jun., or John the 4th, resided in the north-west part of the Farms school-district, in Canton, on land now owned by the heirs of the late Asaph Tuller, Esq. Among his children were the wife of Abraham Barber, Jun., John, Timothy and Dan. The father died May, 1802. The family are now extinct in Canton. Carmi, another son of John Higley, 3d, married Hestor, widow of Thomas Case, 2d, and daughter of Capt. Josiah Case. He was in the American army in the autumn of 1776; was taken a prisoner by the British, and with many others, confined in one of the New York churches, then made a prison of, for the purpose of starving soldiers to death, where he died under British cruelty. He left an infant son of his own name; that son was lost at sea when a man, some forty years of age or more. Obed Higley, son of John Higley, of the fourth degree inclusive from the first John Higley, married Miss Rebecca Mills. He resided most of his family state upon the premises now owned by his son, Alson Higley.

Parents.	Born.	Died.	Age.
Obed Higley,	1757,	1841,	84.
Rebecca Mills,	1766,	1827,	61.

Children.	Born.	Died.	Age.	
Sally,	Sept. 30, 1789,	1815,	26.	Married Allen Case.
Thede,	April 19, 1790,	1853,	63.	Married Benjamin Goff.
Obed,	Jan. 5, 1791.			Married Mary Dickinson.
Alson,	Feb. 20, 1793.			Married Christian Robbins.
Luther,	Nov. 9, 1794.			Married 1st, Electa Woodford; 2d, Flora Bidwell; 3d, Sarah F. Bidwell.
Correl,	Feb. 12, 1796.			Married Nancy Phelps.
Pomeroy,	Nov. 10, 1798.			Married Eunice D. Humphrey.
Amelia,	Oct. 7, 1801.			Married Austin N. Humphrey.
Almenia,	April 1, 1805.			Married Leonard S. Sweett.
Emeline,	Nov. 4, 1808.			Married 1st, Luke Tuller; 2d, Z. Kempton.

NATHANIEL JOHNSON, married Tryphene, daughter of Samuel Barber. He was a joiner by occupation, both for building and shop work; was called an ingenious and faithful workman. His last family residence was on land about one-fourth of a mile north of Gen. E. Hosford's. He had been at work on the house of Mr. Jesse Case, Sen., now the residence of Samuel S. Case. He went into the well to clean the bottom of it, and lost his life by the damps or poisonous air; those who drew his lifeless body from the well, did it with great difficulty, and at the risk of losing their own lives. This event happened September 6th, 1783.

Parents.	Born. Died. Age.
Nathaniel Johnson,	1753, 1783, 30.
Tryphene Barber,	1755.

Children.	Born. Died. Age.	
Chloe,	1777.	Married Charles Adams.
Samuel,	1779.	Married Elizabeth Steele.
Olive,	1781.	Married Medad W. Merrell.
Infant,	1783, 1783.	

JAMES KIRKLAND, with Penelope his wife, resided on a patch of ground on the west side of the road, between Amos L. Spencer and Philetus Case.

Parents.	Born. Died. Age.
James Kirkland,	1736, 1815, 79.
Penelope ——,	1829.

Children.	Born. Died. Age.	
James, Jun.,	1804.	
Cyntha,	1776, 1804, 28.	Married John Philips.
Caleb.		
Jacob.		
Thomas,	1782, 1789. 7.	
Esther,		Married Garner Latimer.

SAMUEL LEETE, was a native of Guilford, a descendant of Gov. William Leete, he married Miss Kelley, of Guilford. They had four children born in Guilford; their names were Jane, who subsequently became the wife of Silas Case, of Canton; she died A. D. 1777 leaving an infant son,

Kelley, who is yet living; Samuel, Jun., born 1766, who married Sarah Case; Amos, born 1769, married Cosmilly Mills; Lucy, an idiot, who died 1793. Mr. Leete, for second wife, married Elizabeth, daughter of Thomas Barber. He removed to Canton and resided on the farm previously owned by Dudley Case, Jun. His house stood on the west side of the road nearly opposite the cooper shop of N. R. L. Bristol, Esq. He died in 1799. Elizabeth, his second wife, died 1825, aged 85.

JONATHAN LATIMER. He settled in the North-east school-district, near Granby line, about the year 1760, on the farm of his late and only son, Jonathan Latimer, late deceased. He had a number of daughters who settled in family state; among them were the first wife of Mr. John Edgerton, who died in the year 1792.

Jonathan Latimer, Sen., died in 1826, aged 91. Mrs. Rachel, his wife, died in 1817, aged 74.

The time of the death of Jonathan Latimer, Jun., or his wife, is not known.

GILES LATIMER, SEN. He settled about 1763, on the farm adjoining to Philetus Case, in the North-east district. He hada number of sons, viz., Giles, Jun., George, Roswell, Garner and James, and a number of daughters.

Mr. Giles Latimer, Sen., died in 1829. His first wife had died in 1808, aged 59. His son, Roswell Latimer, died in 1830, aged 52.

ASA MATSON, SEN. He settled on the place now owned principally by his grandson, Salmon Matson, in the North-east district. His sons were Asa, Jun., William and Joshua; likewise daughters; among them the wife of Elijah Messenger, and the wife of Ezra Paine. The history of this family is but imperfectly known.

HISTORICAL SKETCH OF THE MILLS FAMILY.

In giving some historical sketches of the Mills genealogy herewith appended, it may be proper to state that from common report and investigations carefully made, there were two distinct families of that name who settled in New England, one of English and the other of Dutch descent. Of the latter may be named Rev. Gideon Mills and Rev. Zedekiah Mills, nephews, Rev. Samuel J. Mills and the Rev. Edmund Mills. Of the English descent, tradition says they came from Yorkshire, England. Simon Mills' name first occurs. This Simon Mills married Mary Buel, February 23d, 1649, twenty-nine years after the first settlement of Plymouth. He resided in Windsor previous to 1669, and removed to and settled at Weatauge, East Simsbury. Whether he was a native of New England or not can not be ascertained; one inference is certain, his father was a native of England. This Simon had eleven children, five sons and six daughters; two sons supposed to have died in infancy or in youth.

Children.	Born.	Died.	Age.
Mary,	Dec. 8, 1662.		
Hannah,	1665.		
Simon,	May, 1667.		
John,	Jan. 1668.		
Sarah,	Sept. 1670.		
Abigail,	1672.		
Elizabeth,	1674.		
Prudence,	1676.		
Simon, 2d,	1678.		

JOHN MILLS, son of the last named Simon, was the immediate ancestor of Joseph Mills who settled in West Simsbury. This John Mills married Sarah Pettibone; report says the first ancestor of the Pettibones came from England during Cromwell's wars.

This John Mills had four children, viz., John, Benjamin, Joseph and Sarah. Benjamin and Joseph were twin brothers; Sarah had three husbands, Samuel Tuller, Francis Garrett, Joseph Woodford, whom she survived; children only by the two first.

Mrs. Woodford died in 1797, aged 100 years; her children were noted for their longevity. John Mills the immediate ancestor of the family, died in early life. His surviving widow married Dea. John Humphrey, by whom she had several children, among whom may be named John, Hannah, Benajah, Michael, and Rev. Daniel Humphrey, father of the celebrated Gen. David Humphrey. Joseph Mills, whose record is given, (and grandfather of the compiler* of these historical notes of the family,) was a native of Simsbury, born 1694, and died April 19th, 1783, aged 89 years. At the age of thirty years he married Hannah Adams, aged fifteen years, who was born 1709. She died September 1776, aged 67. They had fourteen children, ten sons and four daughters, all of whom he lived to see married and have children. He removed from Meadow Plain, Old Parish, to West Simsbury, in 1742 or 1743.

Children.	Born. Died. Age.	
Joseph,	1726, 1795, 65.	Had four wives, Lois Case, ———, Remington and Lewis.
Michael,	1728, 1819, 91.	Married Mercy Lawrence.
Hannah,	1731, 1796, 65.	Married Ebenezer Fields.
Samuel,	1734, 1803, 69.	Married ——— Cowles.
Amasa,	1736, 1821, 85.	Married Lucy Curtis.
Benjamin,	1738, 1829, 91.	Married Hannah Humphrey.
Ezekiel,	1740, 1805, 65.	Married Ursula Phelps.
Daniel,	1742, 1779, 37.	
Simeon,	1744, 1778, 34.	

*E. Mills, Esq.

Andrew,	1746, 1813, 67.	Married Naomi Humphrey.
Sarah,	1748, 1805, 57.	Married Joseph Cowles and Asa Foote.
Thankful,	1750, 1776, 26.	Married Charles Wilcox.
Ephraim,	1751, 1818, 67.	Married Rosanna Foote.
Ruth,	1753, 1789, 36.	Married James Andrus.

Average longevity sixty-one and four-fourteenths years.

Without ostentation it may be stated that of the ten sons of which the family were composed, one was colonel of militia, three were captains of military companies, and five were deacons of Congregational churches.

EPHRAIM MILLS, son of Dea. Joseph Mills, and tenth son of the family, was born April 19th, 1751. He had two wives; first wife, Rosanna Foot, daughter of Capt. John Foot; second wife, widow Bethia Johnson, who survived him. He had ten children, seven sons and three daughters. He had children only by his first wife.

He resided on the premises now occupied (1855) by Freeman Case.

Parents.	Born. Died. Age.
Ephraim Mills,	1751, 1818, 67.
1st wife, Rosanna Foot,	1754, 1814, 62.
2d wife, Bethia Johnson.	

Children.	Born. Died. Age.	
Child.		Died in infancy.
Rosanna,	Sept 17, 1780.	Married Arnold P. Humphrey.
Ephraim,	Oct. 19, 1782.	Married 1st, Sarah Case, widow of Orange Case; 2d, Emma Tuller.
Phebe,	March 28, 1784.	Married Stephen Davis.
Simeon,	1786.	Died at the age of 10 months.

Simeon,	Sept. 22, 1787.	Married Anna D. Angilis, Abi Buel, Clarinda Humphrey.
Andrew,	April, 1789.	Died October 14th, 1792, aged 2 years and 6 months.
Ruth,	Nov. 9, 1792.	Married Chauncey G. Griswold.
Andrew,	1793.	Died January 11th, 1804, aged 9 years.
Norman,	Aug. 2, 1795.	Married 1st, Sophia Andrus; 2d Melinda ——.

EPHRAIM MILLS, son of the preceding Ephraim, was born October 19th, 1782; he had two wives. Married January 10th, 1816, Sarah Case, whose maiden name was Jones, widow of Orange Case, who was accidentally killed by the falling of a tree, March 17th, 1814. She was born December 1st, 1783, and died June 4th, 1837, leaving one son, Addison O. Mills, who was born July 14th, 1817.

His second wife was Emma Tuller, daughter of Rufus Tuller. She was born September 28th, 1798. They were married February 28th, 1838. One child, Caroline Emma Mills, was born May 14th, 1840.

Addison O. Mills, above named, married October 17th, 1839. Jane Maria Case, who was born August 7th, 1823, daughter of Capt. Nodiah Case, by whom he has had three children, viz., Sarah Jane, born December 11th, 1844; Addison Nodiah, born March 20th, 1850, and died February 5th, 1853; Ephraim Wilbur, born April 18th, 1854.

Ephraim Mills, now (April, 1855) resides on the premises previously occupied by Zacheus Case, Stephen Harris, and Jacob and Joseph Foote.

Tradition says that Simom Mills, son of the first Simon named in these sketches, when a man, and when the country was infested by lurking and hostile Indians, went into the field to plow, accompanied by two large dogs. An Indian lay in ambush through the day to kill him and take his scalp. Uncle Simon was closely followed by his faithful dogs. The Indian was afraid that unless he killed him outright, uncle Simon would set his dogs upon him, and he would immediately be torn to pieces, which circumstance was the cause of saving Uncle Simon's life. This Indian was afterward taken for murder and executed. At the time of his execution, he disclosed the facts here narrated.

EZEKIEL MILLS, the sixth son of Dea. Joseph Mills. married Ursula Phelps, a native of Hebron, about the year 1762. They resided most of their family state, on the premises now owned by Robert Wilcox, until 1794, when he removed to Becket, Mass. They subsequently removed to the State of Ohio where they both died.

Parents.	Born. Died. Age.
Ezekiel Mills,	1740, 1805, 65.
Ursula Phelps,	1818.

Children.	Born. Died. Age.	
Ursula Clorus,	1763.	Married 1st, Daniel Hitchcock; 2d, Ambrose Cowdry.
Climena,	1766.	Married Robert Wilcox.
Ezekiel Rodolphus,	1768.	Married Orpha Holcomb.
Thomas Delaun,	1770.	Married ——— Lattimer, daughter of Jonathan Lattimer.
Asahel,	1774.	
Oliver.	1777.	
Olive,	1779, 1800, 21.	
Isaac,	1781.	
Roswell,	1783.	

DEA. ANDREW MILLS was the ninth son of Dea. Joseph Mills, born A. D. 1746. He, with his wife Naomi, daughter of Solomon Humphrey, 1st, connected in marriage, about 1771, he resided on the premises now owned by William H. Hallock, Esq. His house was on the site of the house now owned by Rev. Jairus Burt. He removed to Middlebury, State of Vermont, in 1787; was reputed an eminently pious and useful man. In the year 1813, he came on a visit to his native town; was taken sick with typhus fever, and died in the house on the site of the one where he was born aged 67 years.

Parents.	Born. Died. Age.
Andrew Mills.	
Naomi Humphrey,	1749, 1816, 67.

Children.	Born. Died. Age.
Ralph,	1772.
Zenas,	1774.
Louisa,	1776.

CAPT. MICHAEL MILLS. He was the second son of Dea. Joseph Mills, he commenced his first farming operations on the premises now owned by Dea. Lancel Foot. He built his house at the extreme west end of the farm, on the line between him and the heirs of the then late Ephraim Buel, deceased; his house stood some fifty or sixty rods east of the old Cherries Brook road, and north-east of the saw-mill of Humphrey & Brown, in the north part of the Center school-district, there was no open road leading to his house. The old cellar and well are still to be seen. He removed to Norfolk about the year 1772, where his two last sons were born. The farm was sold to Capt. Foot.

Parents.	Born. Died. Age.
Michael Mills,	1728.
Mercy Lawrence.	

Children.	Born.	Died.	Age.
Michael, Jun.	1755.		
Mercy,	1758.		
Ira,	1761.		
Eden,	1763.		
Lawrence,			
Loditha.			
Percy.			
Augustus,	1772.		
Michael Frederick,	1774.		

DEA. BENJAMIN MILLS, the fifth son of Dea. Joseph Mills, Sen. He married Hannah, a daughter of Samuel Humphrey, the third, the first Samuel Humphrey, of West Simsbury. He resided most of his family state on the premises now owned by Alanson Merrills and Harvey Mills, in the West Hill district. He was a captain during most of the campaigns during the Revolutionary war, but never received anything for his time and suffering in the American cause.

He was a man of Christian integrity toward God and his fellow-citizens. His prayers and his pious example will operate long after he is sleeping in the dust, and although he possessed but little of this world's treasure, yet he kept the world indebted to him while he lived in it. The last years of his life he became quite deaf, and his tottering form was permitted to ascend the pulpit, always standing in prayer by the side of the venerable Hallock.

Parents.	Born.	Died.	Age.
Benjamin Mills,	1738,	1829,	91.
Hannah Humphrey,	1740,	1821,	81.

Children.	Born.	Died.	Age.	
Benjamin, 1st,	1757.	1759,	2.	Died in childhood.
Benjamin, 2d,	1759,	1787.	28.	Married Dorcas Case.
Lois,	1761,	1802,	41.	Married John Foot, Jun.

Caina,	1764.	Married Rhoda Case, 2d.
Dudley,	1766.	Married Lovisa Wilcox.
Cyrene,	1769, 1852, 83.	Married Noah Humphrey.
Cosmilly,	1771, 1829, 58.	Married Amos Leete.
Lemuel,	1773, 1808, 35.	Married Dorothy Bodwell.
Thaddeus,	1775, 1846, 71	Married Sarah Case.
Thankful,	1778.	Married Charles Slocum.
Lucretia,	1780, 1809, 29.	Married Plinny Case.
Elizabeth,	1783, 1852, 70.	Died single.
Philemon,	1785, 1793, 8.	Died in youth.

COL. AMASA MILLS, fourth son of Dea. Joseph Mills, with his wife Lucy, the oldest daughter of Peter Curtis, commenced their family state about the year 1756. Their first house was built near where the house of Simeon Mills now stands. He afterward built on the site of the house built by the late Gardner Mills, Sen., deceased, and now occupied by his descendants.

Parents.	Born. Died. Age.
Amasa Mills,	1735, 1821, 86.
Lucy Curtis,	1737, 1816, 79.

Children.	Born. Died. Age.	
Arnon, 1st,	1757.	Died in childhood.
Lucy, 1st.		Died in girlhood.
Lowly,	1760.	Married Job Barber.
Diadama,	1762, 1841, 78.	Married Daniel Merrell.
Amasa, Jun.,	1764, 1846, 82.	Married 1st, Patience Baldwin, 2d, Charlotte Garrett.
Delilah,	1766.	Married Frederick Moses.
Arnon, 2d,	1769, 1810, 41.	Married Mary Barnes.
Lucy, 2d,	1772, 1841, 69.	Married 1st, John Merritt; 2d, David Stockwell.
Gardner,	1773, 1845, 71.	Married Mary F. Skinner.
——,	1775, 1776.	Died in childhood.
Clarissa,	1780, 1792, 12.	Died in early girlhood.

Col. ——— MILLS was a soldier in the old French war on the borders of Canada; he commanded a company in nearly all of the campaigns of the war of the Revolution. He became a major near its close and was a colonel in the militia. He was reputed a good officer and a useful citizen.

Rev. GIDEON MILLS was the seventh son of the first Peter Mills, of Hollandish descent; his wife whose maiden name was Elizabeth, daughter of Brewster Higley, spent the most part of her youth and girlhood in the family of her cousin, the first Gov. Trumbull, of Lebanon. The Rev. Mr. Mills, having been minister of Old Simsbury about ten years previous to 1755, after living and preaching one or two years in West Simsbury, he was installed in the year 1759. He lived and died on the place which was left to his son Gideon, and which after passing through several hands was lately owned by Henry Foote.

All the time of his ministry in West Simsbury, he lived two and a half miles from the meeting-house, over a very hilly, cold and uneven road, which would now be called a hard sabbath day's journey for a clergyman or a layman; this road he traveled weekly, and sometimes much oftener. One incident respecting the Rev. Gideon Mills is thought worthy of notice. He was habitually fond of sacred music, and would request others that could sing to join with him and he retained his relish for singing even to his dying moments. He died of a cancer in the face, which kept him in great suffering, for many of the last weeks of his life. He dwelt much on the sentiments expressed in the 38th psalm, (Watts,) "Amidst thy wrath remember love," &c.; also the 39th. "God of my life look gently down." Just before he expired he requested the friends in attendance to sing the 38th psalm, "Amidst they wrath remember love," and attempted to join with them, but when the fore part of the psalm was sung he expired, so that it was said by Mr. Hallock, on a certain occasion, that he died singing the 38th psalm.

Parents.	Born. Died. Age.	
Rev. Gideon Mills,	1716, 1772, 56.	
Elizabeth Higley,	1723, 1774, 51.	

Children.	Born. Died. Age.	
Gideon, Jun.,	1749, 1813, 64.	
Samuel,	1751, 1814, 63.	Married 1st, Miss Sarah Gilpin; 2d, Miss ——— Belden; 3d, Mrs. ———.
Elizabeth,	1753, 1825, 72.	Married 1st, Gideon Curtis; 2d, Rufus Hawley.
Jedediah,	1755.	Married Miss Wells.
Anna,	1789.	3d wife of Rev. William Robinson.
Faithe,	1765, 1850, 95.	First wife of Roswell Spencer; 2d wife of Eber Alford.

LIEUT. GIDEON MILLS, oldest son of Rev. Gideon and Elizabeth Mills, married Ruth, third daughter of Oliver Humphrey, Esq. He resided on the farm left by his honored father until the year 1800, when he removed to Barkhamsted, where he resided the remainder of his life. They had two sons and four daughters.

Parents.	Born. Died. Age.	
Gideon Mills,	1749, 1813, 64.	Married, 1771.
Ruth Humphrey,	1748, 1822, 74.	

Children.	Born. Died. Age.	
Ruth,	1771, 1808, 37	Married Owen Brown.
Gideon, Jun.,	1773.	Married Dorothy Hayes.
Oliver,	1777.	Married Amelia Wells.
Elizabeth, or Betsy,	1779.	Married Doct. Thompson.
Susannah,	1781.	Married Daniel Richardson.
Sarah Ann.	1783.	Married Daniel Woodruff.

SKETCH OR HISTORY OF THE ANCIENT MILLS FAMILY, THAT WERE BORN AND BROUGHT UP IN WINTONBURY, NOW BLOOMFIELD, AS A DISTINCT RACE FROM THE MILLS OF SIMSBURY AND CANTON.

PETER MILLS, the great ancestor of that race of Mills, came from Holland. Tradition is that his Dutch name before settling in this country was something like Van Molan, which was changed to Mills. He was born 1666, and died 1754, aged 88. He resided near the east part of what is now Bloomfield, eastward from the residence of Samuel Mills, near the confines of Windsor Plain. He was by trade a tailor, which business he followed through the active part of his life. He had seven sons; their names were Jedediah, who graduated at Yale College, A. D. 1722; entered the ministry, and settled in the part of Stratford then called Ripton, now Huntington. He was a minister of considerable note in that period; some of his works were published. He was the ancestor of the Mills in Fairfield and New Haven counties. Pelatiah, another son, was born 1693, and was an able attorney at law, and useful citizen, and was the ancestor of the Mills now remaining in Bloomfield and Windsor. John, another son, was the father of Rev. Samuel John, and Rev. Edmund, minister of Sutton, Mass. Peter was the father of a numerous offspring scattered in various parts of the country; among them Mrs. Anna Hinman; now living in Canton; Rev. Ebenezer, graduate of 1739, first minister of East Granby. His descendants are in Sandisfield and vicinity. Rev. Gideon, the seventh son, graduated at Yale College, A. D. 1737; settled in Simsbury first, afterward in West Simsbury. (See history of Rev. Gideon Mills.) There was in the early part of the family, one by the name of Return, about whom very little is now known further than the record that she died A. D. 1689. Pelatiah, 2d, a grandson of Peter, was a man held in high estimation, both in civil, ecclesiastical, and religious concerns. He died, 1786.

Rev. SAMUEL MILLS, son of Rev. Gideon Mills, commenced study in early life with a view to the gospel ministry. He graduated at Yale College, A. D. 1776. Being full of the patriotism prevalent at that time, he entered the American army as lieutenant in the cavalry. In one of those actions which took place in the autumn of 1777, this young officer received a wound from a horseman's sword, in the forehead; was taken prisoner and conveyed into Philadelphia, with a deep and dangerous wound, the scar of which he carried through the remainder of his life, The sick and wounded prisoners in Philadelphia, experienced far different treatment from that which those unfortunate American prisoners received from the British and Tories in New York in 1776. A kind Providence furnished a goodly number of ministering angels, (if the expression might be allowable,) in the persons of some of the most accomplished ladies of Philadelphia. Those of superior rank and refinement, took it upon them to visit and minister to the wants of the suffering prisoners. Among those worthy ladies was Miss Sarah Gilpin, a person of high refinement and accomplishments. Her labors of benevolence, brought her and Lieut. Samuel to an acquaintance, which eventuated in his obtaining her hand and heart. He pursued and finished his theological studies, and was married to Miss Gilpin, and was settled pastor over the church and society of Chester, then a part of Saybrook. She was the mother of eight children. Their names were Mary, Samuel, Thomas Sarah, Emily, Gideon John, Eliza and Benoni. She died in 1796. Mr. Mills, in the year 1798, married Miss Rebecca Belden, daughter of Col. John Belden, of Wethersfield. They had one son, born in 1800. The mother died in 1801. Mr. Mills afterward married his third wife, with whom he lived till 1814, when he died of typhus fever, which was then prevalent in that town. Mrs. Mills, the third wife, died but a few days after him, of the same disease.

JOHN MILLS, Jun., was born 1690, and was son of John Mills, Sen., and brother to Dea. Joseph Mills, of West Simsbury. He with his wife Damaris Phelps, married 1720, and resided on the land at the junction of the lovely street road with the Hartford and Albany turnpike, near the old Hosford stand. They had four sons, Job, John, David and Jared; also a daughter Prudence, who was married to Samuel Humphrey, 4th.

JARED MILLS' FAMILY.

Parents.	Born.	Died.	Age.	
Jared Mills,	Oct. 8, 1746,	1822,	76.	Married March 11th, 1767.
1st wife, Apphia Higley,	1746,	1783,	37.	
2d wife, Joannah Russell,	1743,	1820,	67.	Married March 17th, 1784.
3d wife, Ann Dyer,		1843,	91.	Married July 19th, 1821.

Children.	Born.	Died.	Age.	
Lucretia,	Dec. 11, 1767,	1771,	3.	
A son,	Aug. 20, 1769.			Lived but a short time.
Chloe,	July 14, 1770,	1838,	68.	Married Frederick West.
Jared, Jr.,	Dec. 19, 1772,	1821,	49.	Married 1st, Susannah Case; 2d, Polly Fowler.
Joel,	Feb. 10, 1775,	1776,	1.	
Joel, 2d,	Dec. 3, 1776,	1823,	47.	Married Joanna Russell, 2d.
Daughter,	Dec. 13, 1778.			Lived but a short time.
A son,	Aug. 29, 1779.			
Daughter,	July 20, 1780.			
A son,	Dec. 1, 1781.			
Norman,	Sept. 30, 1784,	1824,	40.	Married Charlotte Laflin.
Lucretia,	Jan. 27, 1786,	1817,	31.	
Isaac,	Aug. 7, 1787.			Living, 1856; married Assenath Merrill.
Harriet,	Feb. 9, 1789.			Living, 1856; married Joseph Daily.
Catharine,	March 27, 1790.			Living, 1856; married Samuel Pettibone.

Damaris,	Dec. 25, 1791, 1792, 1.	
Damaris,	June 13, 1793.	Married Cyrus Miller.
George,	Feb. 26, 1795.	Married Betsy Woodford.

JOHN MOSES. He was among the earliest settlers in the Northern part of West Simsbury, probably as early as 1745. He, with his wife Rhoda, settled on the place now owned by Seymour D. Moses, in the North district, near the North burying-ground, which was on his premises. His little daughter Eunice was the first that was interred in that place. She died March, 1754, aged two years and four months. He subsequently removed to the premises now owned by Robert Case and sons. He erected a grist mill on his last farm, which bore his name. He left the town in the latter part of the last century, and but little is known respecting his last years or of his family.

Parents.	Born. Died. Age.	
John Moses.		
Rhoda,	1725, 1768, 43.	
Children.	Born. Died. Age.	
Eunice,	1752, 1754, 2.	
Rhoda,	1756, 1761, 5.	
Infant,	1768, 1768.	Aged 1 month.

BENONI MOSES. He, with his wife Susannah, settled in the North district on lands now owned by Anson Case, about the year 1744. He was a carpenter by trade, and a man of considerable note. There is but little known about this family now, except by tradition and by burial list.

Parents.	Born. Died. Age.	
Benoni Moses,	1711, 1787, 76.	
1st wife, Susannah,	1719, 1774, 55.	Daughter of John Humphrey, Esq.
2d wife, Phebe,	1726. 1786, 60.	

Children.	Born. Died. Age.	
Ezekiel,	1741.	
Elnathan,	1743.	
Susannah,	1746.	
Lois,	1749.	Married Darius Hill.
Shubael,	1753.	
Sarah,	1756.	
Ezekiel, 2d,	1762.	
Elizabeth,	1765.	

LIEUT. TIMOTHY MOSES died 1793, aged 62 years. Thankful, his wife, died 1790, aged 59 years.

ELISHA MOSES, a brother of Aaron, came with his wife to West Simsbury and settled in the North district in 1757, on the farm now owned by Eliphalet Case. They had four children, including one that died in infancy. His wife was a daughter of Thomas and Mercy Barber; the latter died at the house of her daughter, in 1793, aged 93 years.

Parents.	Born. Died. Age.
Elisha Moses,	1736, 1808, 71.
Mercy Barber,	1815.

Children.	Born. Died. Age.	
Mercy,	1762.	Married Elihu Beach.
Elisha,	1760.	Married Miss Merrells.
Infant,	1764, 1764.	
Frederick,	1769, 1824, 55.	Married Delilah Mills.

DEA. AARON MOSES, a son of Timothy Moses, with his wife, Susannah Seymour, came from Wintonbury to West Simsbury, about the year 1757, and settled in the North district, on the premises now (1856) owned by Thomas and Horace Vining. They had six children.

Parents.	Born. Died. Age.	
Aaron Moses,	1733, 1809, 76.	
1st wife, Susannah Seymour,	1738, 1783, 45.	
2d wife, Rachel Gilbert,	1732, 1821, 89.	

Children.	Born. Died. Age	
Darius,	1758, 1824, 66.	Married Sarah Adams.
Aseneth,	1760.	Married —— Adams.
Susannah,	1762.	Married Joseph Buttolph.
Aaron Seymour,	1763, 1772, 9.	
Martin Levi,	1767, 1784, 17.	He was drowned.
Seymour Aaron,	1772, 1846, 74.	Married Rhoda Humphrey.

CAPT. **DARIUS MOSES**, son of Dea. Aaron and Susannah, and grandson of Lieut. Timothy Moses. He resided and erected the dwelling-house and buildings on the premises now owned by Stanley Weed, in the North school-district. He was a very useful citizen.

Parents.	Born. Died. Age.	
Darius Moses,	1758, 1824, 66.	
Sarah Adams,	1755, 1834, 79.	Daughter of Lieut. David Adams.

Children.	Born. Died. Age.	
Sarah,	1780, 1854, 74.	Died single.
Darius, 2d,	1782, 1824, 42.	Married Sodema Holcomb, daughter of Jesse Holcomb.
Ashbel,	1784.	Married Candace Dyer.
Roxy,	1786, 1788, 2.	Died by being scalded.
Chauncey,	1789, 1851, 62.	Married Katherine Johnson.
Flora,	1791.	Married Elisha Sugden.
Roxy,	1796.	Married Bela Squires.
Chester,	1798.	Married Charlotte Moses.

ABRAHAM MOSES, son of Caleb Moses, Jun., of Simsbury was married to Mercy, daughter of Richard and Mary Case. They resided on land now belonging to John Case, situated between the farms of Nelson Aldrich and Roswell Barnes, on the East Hill. He made a public profession of religion in advanced life, A. D. 1821, being a subject of the revival of that year. He appeared to honor his profession during the brief period of his subsequent life. He died in the summer of 1823, in his barn and alone. From appearance, viewing the place and posture in which he was found, it was believed that death found him praying.

Parents.	Born.	Died.	Age.	
Abraham Moses,		1823.		
Mercy Case,	1752,	1818,	66.	
Children.	**Born.**	**Died.**	**Age.**	
Loditha.				Married Joab Barber.
Abraham, Jun.,		1802,	29.	Married Charlotte Alford.
Mercy.				Married William Rowland.
Dorcas.				Married Job Talbot, of Avon.
James.				Married Clarissa Wilcox.
Thaddeus,		1828,	44.	Married Mereb Brockway; she died in 1845, aged 58.

DANIEL MOSES, son of Caleb Moses, He, with his wife, who was Mary Wilcox, a daughter of Azariah Wilcox, came from the Old Parish to West Simsbury about the year 1756, and settled on the farm now owned by Bethuel Case, adjoining the farm of the late Capt. Robert Wilcox, deceased, in North Canton. They had three sons and three daughters, besides two that died in childhood, about the year 1770.

Parents.	Born.	Died.	Age.	
Daniel Moses,		1776.		Died in the army.
Mary Wilcox,	1732,	1816,	84.	

Children.	Born. Died. Age.	
Daniel, Jun.,	1758, 1805, 47.	Married Anna Edgerton.
Zebina,	1815, 51.	Married Theodosia Curtis.
———.		Married Andrew Roby.
———.		Married Martin Roberts.
Roger,	1828.	Married Patience T. Barber.
Charlotte.		Married Job Phelps.

ICHABOD MILLER. He, with his wife Sarah Holcomb, removed from the Old Parish to West Simbury about the year 1746. They settled on the farm that had been left by Mr. Ephraim and Mrs. Mercy Buel, both deceased. The farm was adjoining Thomas Barber's. There were nine children in this Miller family.

Parents.	Born. Died. Age.
Ichabod Miller,	1703, 1793, 90.
Sarah Holcomb,	1716, 1800, 84.

Children.	Born. Died. Age.	
Dudley, 1st,	1742, 1762, 20.	He died at Havana,
Aaron,	1744.	He removed to Vermont.
Samuel,	1746.	He removed to State of New York.
Sarah,	1749.	Married John Merritt.
Mehittabel,	1752.	
Sabra,	1755, 1807, 52.	Married George Adams.
Ruth,	1757.	
Moses,	1760.	Married Ruth, a daughter of Richard Case, and removed to Hudson, Ohio.
Dudley, 2d.	1762, 1787, 25.	

DUDLEY MILLER, 2D, was executed in 1787, in the State of New York. The crime was forgery, which, by a law of that State was punished by death.

MR. ICHABOD MILLER and a Mr. Eliot, had the charge of the works erected in Simsbury for the manufacture of steel, about the year 1743. (See *Phelps' History*, p. 88.) His blacksmith's shop in this town stood a few rods north of the saw mill lately erected by Humphrey & Brown. He occupied this place probably from twelve to sixteen years, and then removed to what is now West Granby, where he died. His remains were brought to Canton and interred in the North burying-ground.

JAMES McNALL, (the descendants will now have it to be McNEAL,) was of Irish descent. He married Mindwell, a daughter of Gamaliel Ward After the death of his father-in-law, and the death and removal of the other members of the Ward family, he remained a resident of the Ward place, so called, till he removed from West Simsbury, about A. D. 1794. The Ward farm was situated in the North school-district, is now part of the western end of the premises of Eliphalet Case. The house stood the west side of the highway, some six or eight rods north of the bridge that crosses Cherries brook. The time of birth or death of the parents can not be ascertained.

Children.	Born.	Died.	Age.
Rebecca, or Betsy.			
James, Jun.,	1767.		
Alexander,	1770.		
Calvin, and a twin that died,	1774.		
Luther,	1776.		
Eunice,	1779.		
Roxy,	1781.		

JONATHAN MERRELL, SEN. He came from West Hartford about the year 1739, and settled on the place afterward owned by Dudley Case, and now owned by the family of Mrs. Olive Pike. He had three sons and two daughters who settled in family state, and four of them had families. Jonathan Merrell, Sen., died in 1788, aged about 90 years.

Children.	Born. Died. Age.	
William,	1732, 1806, 74.	Married Sarah Kellogg.
Jonathan, Jun.,	1734.	Married Hannah Douglass.
Hepzibah,	1743, 1817, 74.	Married 1st, William Humphrey; 2d. Sylvanus Case.
George.		
Susannah,	1741, 1810, 69.	Married Dudley Case, Jun.

WILLIAM MERRELL, SEN., son of Jonathan Merrell, Sen. He with his wife, who was Sarah Kellogg, settled on the place that was afterward owned by the late Capt. Isaac Merrell. He settled in family state about the year 1752.

Parents.	Born. Died. Age.
William Merrell,	1732, 1806, 74.
Sarah Kellogg,	1735, 1801, 66.

Children.	Born. Died. Age.	
Sarah,	1752.	Married Oliver Bronson, the the father of Judge Greene C. Bronson, of New York.
——,	1754, 1786, 32.	Married Ashbel Benham.
Rhoda,	1757, 1792, 37.	
Daniel,	1759, 1829, 70.	Married Diadama Mills.
William, Jun.,	1761, 1830, 69.	Married 1st, Elizabeth Wilcox; 2d, Thede Brown.
Sybil,	1763.	Married Asa Cowles.
Margaret,	1765.	Married William Roberts.
Isaac,	1767, 1846, 78.	Married Elizabeth Seymour; died, 1855.
Candace,	1771.	Married Bates Willey.

JONATHAN MERRELL, 2D, with his wife, who was Hannah Douglass, settled on the premises now owned by Norman N. Bidwell. They had three sons and four daughters who settled in family state and left children.

Parents.	Born. Died. Age.
Jonathan Merrell,	1734.
Hannah Douglass,	1741.

Children.		Born. Died. Age.	
Rachael,	April,	1763.	Married 1st, ——— Miller, who was drowned; 2d. James Hill.
Jonathan, Jun.,		1764, 1842, 78.	Married 1st, Asenath Tuller; 2d, widow Goodwin.
Benajah,	June,	1766.	Married Mrs. ——— Henderson.
Abi,	Jan.,	1769, 1848, 79.	Married Jonathan Barber.
Hannah,	March,	1772, 1816, 44.	Married Roswell Barnes.
Susannah,	Nov.,	1773.	
George,	Dec.,	1778, 1842, 64.	

GEORGE MERRELL, son of Jonathan Merrell, 1st, settled at first on the place in New Hartford, (now Canton;) the farm is now owned by the family of Mrs. Olive Pike; afterward he removed from it to the farm that was the property of the late Daniel Merrell, deceased.

This family have long been gone from this part of the country.

Children.	Born. Died. Age.	
Hannah,	1806.	Married Chauncey Pettibone.
———,		Married Edward Dill.
Shubael.		

JOSEPH MESSENGER, was the first of that name that settled in West Simsbury, and was a son of Nathan Messenger, of Windsor. Joseph Messenger, and his wife, Catharine Holcomb, daughter of Nathaniel Holcomb, and granddaughter of Thomas, Holcomb, came from that part of Simsbury that is now Granby, and settled in West Simsbury in 1742, in the north-west part of the Center school-district; his son Isaac and his wife came with them. They settled on the farm now owned by Almon and Newel Messenger.

Parents.	Born. Died. Age.	
Joseph Messenger.	1685, 1763, 78.	Married, 1707.
Katharine Holcomb,	1689, 1769, 80.	

Children.	Born. Died. Age.
Sarah,	1710.
Joseph, Jun.,	1713.
Jehiel,	1715.
Isaac,	1717.
Catharine,	1720.
Elijah,	1722.
Nathaniel,	1725.

ISAAC MESSENGER. was the third son of Joseph and Katherine Messenger. He settled on the farm that was occupied by his father. Isaac and his wife had fifteen children, ten sons and five daughters; thirteen of the family grew up and settled in life, and twelve of them left children.

Mr. Isaac Messenger was in the early part of his family state, an expert hunter. His family were noted as being remarkably large, strong and robust.

Parents.	Born. Died. Age.	
Isaac Messenger,	1717, 1801, 84.	
Hannah Alford,	1727, 1811, 84.	Daniel of Nathaniel Alford.

Children.	Born. Died. Age.	
Joseph, Jr.,	1741.	Married Jemima Barber.
Hannah,	1743.	Married William Brittian.
Isaac.	1745.	Married Anna Ward.
Simeon,	1746, 1821, 75.	Married Mary Paine.
Moses,	1748, 1811, 63.	Married Isabel McFarland.
Aaron,	1750.	
Reuben,	1752, 1838, 86.	Married Eunice Bunce.
Dorcas,	1754, 1760, 6.	
Elisha,	1756.	Married —— Hayes.
Elijah,	1758.	Married Lucretia Matson.
Abner,	1760.	Married Abigail Pike.
Dorcas,	1762, 1793, 31.	Married William Brittian.
Rosy,	1764, 1849, 85.	Married Francis Bacon.
Keziah,	1766, 1778, 12.	
Carmi,	1771, 1825, 54.	Married 1st, Rachel Daniels; 2d, Sabra Case.

JOSEPH MESSENGER, 3D, oldest son of Isaac Messenger, grandson of Joseph, 1st, and great grandson of Nathan Messenger, of Windsor, married to Jemima Barber, daughter of the then late Jonathan Barber, deceased, commenced family state about the year 1762; was the first resident on the farm afterward owned by Theophilus Humphrey, adjoining Kimberley's line. This farm is now owned by Loin H. Humphrey, and occupied by John Millard, Esq. He removed in 1782, to Otis, Mass., and removed from Otis about 1791, to the Delaware region, State of Pennsylvania, where it is understood he spent the remainder of his life. Among his children were Joseph, Jun., Cornish, Jemima, Zebina, and perhaps others. This is all that is known to the writer about this family.

ISAAC MESSENGER, JUN., was second son of Isaac, Sen. He married Anna, daughter of Gamaliel Ward. He, in the early part of his family state, resided on the farm now owned and occupied by Friend White, within the confines of Barkhamsted, in the part then called Ratlum. He removed from Barkhamsted to Western New York, about the year 1794. His children were Isaac, Jun., Hannah, Damaris, and others, including some four that died in infancy.

SIMEON MESSENGER. He was the third son of Isaac, Sen. He, with his wife, settled in the year 1769, on the Hill farm, then in the town of New Hartford. The site of his first house was near the dwelling now occupied by Daniel Humphrey, near the confines of Barkhamsted. His first house was destroyed by fire in 1785, but was rebuilt soon and he remained there until 1792, when he removed to the south-east part of Barkhamsted, where he spent the remainder of his life. He was a man of great frame, large bone, and of great strength for labor, when in the prime of life particularly at mowing. It may be said of the whole of those ten Messenger brothers, that they were uncommonly great, strong men.

Parents.	Born. Died. Age.	
Simeon Messenger,	1746, 1821, 75.	
Mary Paine,	1825.	
Children.	**Born. Died. Age.**	
Betsy,	1770.	Married Noah Gibbert.
Hira,	1772.	Died single.
Simeon, Jun.,	1773.	Married Lucy Daniels.
Trueman,	1775.	Moved to State of New York.
Loditha,	1777.	Married 1st, John Wright; 2d, Avery Brown.
Diadama,	1779, 1830, 51.	Married John Higley.
William,	1781.	Married Ruth Miller.
Elihu,	1783.	Married Polly Merritt.

JOHN OWEN, the great ancestor of most of the Owens, was a native of Wales, Great Britain. He was among the first settlers of Windsor. He married Rebecca Wade, A. D. 1650. Their children were, Josias, born 1651; then two in succession by the name of John, who both died in childhood; Nathaniel, born 1656; Daniel, born 1658; Joseph, born 1660; Mary, born 1662; Benjamin, born 1664. The late John Owen, Esq., of Simsbury, was a descendant of Josias, one of the aforementioned sons. Isaac Owen married Sarah Holcomb. They had two sons. Isaac, Jun., or 2d, was the ancestor of the Owens in Turkey Hills, or East Granby. Elijah, the second son of the first Isaac, and grandson of the first John Owen, was the ancestor of another family of Owens, who removed to the State of Massachusetts; also, a family of Alfords, the children of Benedict Alford and Rebecca Owen who removed to Vermont about 1790; also of Hannah, the wife of Capt. John Brown, the mother of the Brown family that were reared up in Canton the latter part of the last century.

CAPT. ABRAHAM PETTIBONE, SEN., son of Samuel Pettibone, Jun., and great grandson of the first John Pettibone, was an early settler in West Britain, now Burlington. His landed property lay on the confines of Burlington, New Hartford and Canton. He is entitled to a place in these short sketches, as numbers of his descendants were connected with, and became inhabitants of Canton, and there lie buried the remains of the early fathers, and mothers, of their race. He, for first wife, married Jerusha Pinney, of Simsbury; for second, daughter of Dea. Michael Humphrey, and widow of Lieut. Sadosa Wilcox.

Parents.	Born. Died. Age.	
Abraham Pettibone,	1727, 1797, 70.	
Children by 1st wife.	Born. Died. Age.	
Abraham, Jun.,	1751, 1834, 83.	Married 1st, Amelia Smith; 2d, Huldah Prindle.

Jerusha,	1753, 1815, 62.	Married Seth Spencer, of New Hartford.
Samuel,	1755, 1778, 23.	Died aboard of prison-ship in New York.
Elizabeth,	1756, 1784, 28.	Married George Humphrey.
Theodore,	1761, 1821, 60.	Married Mary Humphrey.
Chauncey,	1766, 1801, 35.	Married Hannah Merrell.
Alexander,	1763, 1801, 38.	Married Lydia Humphrey.
Charlotte,	1772, 1855, 83.	Married Joseph Dyer.
Theophilus,	1769, 1834, 65.	Married Esther Whitmore.
Norman,	1774, 1814, 40.	Married 1st Lovisa Nobles, of Westfield, Mass.; 2d. Pamelia Whitmore.

Children by 2d wife.	Born. Died. Age.	
Clarissa,	1784.	Married Horatio Gates, of Douglass, Mass.; now living, (1856.)
Roxy,	1782, 1848, 66.	Married John Beckwith.
Anna,	1786, 1822, 36.	Married Norman Humphrey.

THOMAS PHELPS settled in West Simsbury, (now Canton,) in the year 1745. He first resided on the place now owned by Richard Case. His wife, Margaret Watson, a near relative (supposed to be aunt) of the noted James Watson, who flourished in New York in the latter part of the Eighteenth century, and was noted for enterprise, wealth and respectability.

Parents.	Born. Died. Age.
Thomas Phelps,	1710, 1777, 67.
Margaret Watson,	1717, 1777, 60.

Children.	Born. Died. Age.	
Sarah,	1738.	2d wife of Hezekiah Adams.
Thomas,	1740, 1789, 49.	Was father of the late Anson G. Phelps, of New York; married Dorothy Woodbridge, granddaughter of Rev. Timothy Woodbridge.

Margaret,	1745.	Married Moses Cook.
Lois,	1747, 1776, 29.	2d wife of Daniel Graham.
Hannah,	1749, 1825, 76.	Married James Merritt.
Job,	1752, 1777, 24.	Married Phebe ——.
Mary,	1755, 1784, 29.	Married Joel Barber.

BENJAMIN PHELPS, brother of Thomas Phelps, with Lydia Palmer, his first wife, came from Windsor to West Simsbury, about the year ——. He lived on the place now owned by Richard Case.

Parents.	Born. Died. Age.
Benjamin Phelps,	1718, 1785, 67.
1st wife, Lydia Palmer,	1740, 1776, 36.
2d wife, Elizabeth Goodhue,	1812.

Children by 1st wife.	Born. Died. Age.	
Benjamin, Jun.,	1769, 1775, 6.	
Lydia,	1770, 1802, 31.	Married Freeman Graham.
Sarah,	1776, 1776.	

Children by 2d wife	Born. Died, Age.	
Elizabeth,	1780, 1832, 52.	
Benjamin,	1782, 1850, 68.	Died in the State of New York.

WILLIAM PAINE settled on the place now owned by Elijah Whiting, about the year 1758. He had sons of the names of Jesse, Isaac, Abraham, Ezra and Eber. The names of the daughters are not known to the writer. The family removed out of West Simsbury on to the farm now owned by Dea. Charles Richards, of New Hartford.

JOB PHELPS, son of Thomas, Sen., and Margaret Phelps, married Phebe ———, about 1772. The wife and mother died in 1776, aged 20. He resided on the east side of the road, east of the house now owned by the family of the late Robert Case, Jun., deceased. After the death of his wife he went into the army; was camp waiter to Capt. John Brown, in 1776, and died of small-pox in 1777.

Parents.	Born. Died. Age.
Job Phelps,	1752, 1777, 24.
Phebe ———,	1756, 1776, 20.
Children.	**Born. Died. Age.**
Job, Jun., or 2d.	1772.
Infant,	1775, 1775.

GEORGE PHELPS, with William, his brother, came from England. George was the great ancestor of Thomas and Benjamin Phelps. The descent from George to Thomas was followed down through, by the name of three Abrahams, in direct succession.

DARIUS PRIEST and Hepzibah ———, his wife, resided in West Simsbury as early as 1768. He resided on several different farms during his life; was a remarkably strong man for labor; his two oldest children were cut down in the autumn of 1776, by the dysentery, which was then prevalent and very mortal in this part of the country.

Parents.	Born. Died. Age.
Darius Priest,	1744, 1801, 57.
Hepzibah ———,	1751, 1801, 50.
Children.	**Born. Died. Age.**
Cyntha,	1769, 1776, 7.
Mary,	1772, 1776, 4.

Darius, Jun.,	1775.	
William,	1778.	
Hepzibah.	1787, 1806, 19,	Was living with Mr. Hosea Case.

WILLIAM ROBERTS, 1st. There were among the early settlers of West Simsbury, two by the name of William Roberts. It is not known what relationship they sustained to each other, if any. They will be here distinguished in this work by the term of 1st and 2d. William Roberts, 1st, was among the pioneers of the town of Canton. His residence was on land, now the east part of the farm of Israel W. Graham. His wife was Hannah ———. They probably had several children, but nothing is known to the writer except what follows, viz., their daughter Anna, who was born in 1748, became the wife of Abel Adams. Record te lls us also, that Mr. and Mrs. Roberts buried a daughter Susannah, born in 1756, and died the same year. The parents, about the time of the commencement of the American Revolution, removed to the State of Vermont, which closes their history as it respects Canton.

WILLIAM ROBERTS, 2d, commenced family state, with his wife Phebe Wilcox, about 1756. They resided in the vicinity of the village of Collinsville. He lost his life in attempting to cross the dam at Segur's mill, at low water. An axe that he was known to have with him when he was last seen, was found near the dam, although his body had floated down stream many rods. His death happened about the year 1774. His widow afterward married John Wallen, of New Hartford.

Parents.	Born. Died. Age.
William Roberts, 2d.	
Phebe Wilcox.	

Children.	Born. Died, Age.	
Martin.		Married a daughter of the late Daniel Moses.
William, Jun.,	1824.	Married Margaret Merrill; she died, 1824.
Phebe,	1837, 76.	Married Riverius Bidwell, Esq.
Lucina,	1816.	Married David Taylor.
Reuben,	1789.	Died unmarried.
Mindwell,	1833, 64.	Married Gurdon Humphrey, father of the late Mrs. Eliza Spencer.
Elizabeth,	1844.	Married William Humphrey.
Aseneth.		Married Thomas Gleason.

HEZEKIAH RICHARDS, with his wife, whose maiden name was Sarah Case, settled at the south-west part of West Simsbury, near the confines of New Hartford and Burlington. He resided on the premises now owned by his grandson, William J. Richards. They had five children, four sons and one daughter. The time of their settlement in West Simsbury was A. D. 1761.

Parents.	Born. Died. Age.
Hezekiah Richards,	1732, 1776, 44.
Sarah Case.	1734, 1799, 65.

Children.	Born. Died. Age.	
Hezekiah, Jun.,	1757, 1831, 74.	Married 1st, Miss Moses; 2d, ———.
Timothy,	1760, 1782, 22.	
Samuel,	1763, 1837, 74.	Married 1st, Ede Case; 2d, Naomi Simons.
Sarah,	1766, 1853, 87,	Married Michael Braughton.
Jonah,	1769, 1850, 81.	Married Nancy Cornwall.

THOMAS SUGDEN came from England as a soldier in the British army. It is understood that he deserted from the British service. He came to Connecticut in 1777, and married Persia Dunham, of New Britain, where he commenced family state, but soon removed to the south-west part of Simsbury, Old Parish; from the latter place he in 1802, removed to Canton, North school-district, and settled on the place now owned by Marvin Case.

Parents.	Born. Died. Age.	
Thomas Sugden,	1759, 1819, 60.	
Persia Dunham,	1759, 1834, 75.	

Children.	Born. Died. Age.	
John,	1780.	Married Elizabeth Hull.
Thomas, Jun.,	1783.	Married Thede Humphrey; removed to Hartland in 1812, then to Michigan in 1833.
Elisha,	1786, 1843, 57.	Married Flora Moses; removed to Hartford in 1838, where he died in 1843.
Sarah, or Sally,	1788.	Married Elisha Pettibone.
Hannah,	1790, 1808, 18.	Died single.
Nancy.	1792.	Married David Taylor.
Chester,	1796, 1815, 19.	Died single.

JOHN SEGUR, with his first wife Elizabeth, came from the east part of Simsbury, and settled in West Granby, adjoining the premises of Noah and Levi Case, about the year 1750.

Parents.	Born. Died. Age.	
John Segur,	1725, 1808, 83.	
1st wife, Elizabeth,	1729, 1760, 31.	Her infant was buried with her.
2d wife, Huldah,	1785.	
3d wife, Deliverance Clarke,	1728. 1801. 73.	

Children.	Born.	Died.	Age.	
Elizabeth,		1795.		Married Jesse Steele,
Annah,	1758,	1779,	21.	
Infant,	1760,	1760.		
John.				Died young.
Augustus,		1839.		Married daughter of Eli Tuller.
Huldah.				
Two infants,	1768,	1768.		
Mary,	1770,	1779,	9.	

JOSEPH SEGUR, JUN., was an early settler in West Simsbury. He resided on the west side of Farmington river. His house stood where is now the center of Collinsville, west village. The farm that he owned, now belongs to the Collins Company, and Samuel W. Collins, Esq. During a great share of his family state previous to 1795, he tended the grist-mill, then called Segur's Mill. The mill stood the east side of the river some eight or ten rods south of the main bridge, the great flat rock in the middle of the river, making the middle part of the dam, which was a low one. He daily crossed the river in his canoe, to go to and from the grist-mill, when the river was not frozen sufficient to be safe crossing on the ice. Among his children were Israel, Charles, Benoni, the wife of Eliphalet Alford, and two other daughters. He, with his son Benoni, removed to New Hartford in 1805, to spend the remainder of his days, where he and his wife died in 1818. The family are now gone from this town. His father Joseph Segur, Sen., married Dorothy Alford in 1730. The writer will relate one little incident connected with that mill, which made some sport among the people at the time being. Mr. Chauncey Gleason, a trader in the East Village, then called Suffrage, having a quantity of brimstone in the roll or lump, wishing to pulverize it into fine sulphur, (an article sometimes used in families at that time,) carried a large quantity of it to Segur's mill to be ground, in the year 1789-90; it was put into the corn-mill, but it soon took fire and flamed up frightfully. Gleason ran to the river and brought water in his hat to extinguish the flames. The undertaking soon proved a failure, and in the operation, Mr. Gleason having on a valuable broadcloth coat, spoiled it for use; the mill became thoroughly scented with the itch antidote, and the event was well spread abroad. A neighboring poor family had a small grist of indian corn ground in the mill afterward, and in trying to bake some of the meal in johnny cakes before the fire, their cakes ignited and blazed up. A man by the name of Bethuel Parker, an apt poetical genius, wrote a lengthy and apt poem on this laughable subject, entitled "Hell upon Earth, or Brimstone in the Grist-Mill," touching upon different parts of the scene, something after the manner of Cowper's John Gilpin. He compared the blazing of the mill and johnny cakes, to Mount Ætna in a blaze. The closing lines were:

"Then Segur cries out in bitterness of soul,
Have mercy, Lord, though I did take large toll."

CALEB SPENCER, with his wife Hannah ——, came from Hartford, and first settled and built near the dwelling-house of the late Giles Lattimer. He subsequently bought of Daniel Barber, of Simsbury, and lived and died on the place now owned by his great grandson, Amos L. Spencer, North Canton. He settled in this town about 1756.

Parents.	Born. Died. Age.	
Caleb Spencer,	1735, 1816, 81.	
Hannah Spencer,	1735, 1798, 63.	
Children.	**Born. Died. Age.**	
Ebenezer,	1760.	Married Betsey Little.
Roswell,	1806.	Married Faith Mills.
Caleb,	1762, 1770, 8.	
Moses,	1768, 1770, 2.	
Amos,	1772, 1847, 75.	Married Candace Case.
Hannah, about	1775.	Married George Lattimer.

——— SMITH, married a daughter of Nathaniel Alford, 1st. He, with his brother-in-law, Joseph Tiff, resided away from the road, south of the John Hill farm, near the south end of the east mountain. He was known by the vulgar name of Noggy Smith. He removed to Vermont about A. D. 1786.

JOSEPH TIFF, with his wife Susan, daughter of Nathaniel Alford, 1st, lived with his brother-in-law Smith, on the East Hill. The family have long been gone from this town. This is all that can now be ascertained respecting these two families, that had a place among the first settlers.

SOLOMON THOMAS was an early settler in West Simsbury. He, with his wife Lugia, lived on the place now owned by Miles and Mills Foot. His son Samuel lived with them. They both removed to Otis, Mass., about the year 1798, where the old gentleman died the beginning of the present century, aged about 90. His wife had died in the year 1779; she was also daughter of Nathaniel Alford, 1st. But little more is known about this family.

WILLIAM TAYLOR, with his second wife Ruth, the widow of ——— Higgins, came from Middletown about the year 1756, and settled on premises now owned by Alson Barber. They both had previously been married to other partners, and he had children, John and Mary, and probably others. She, by her first marriage, had Nathaniel Higgins, who died in 1809, aged 60 years. The time of the birth, death, or age, of Mr. Taylor's first children is not known. Mr. Taylor, in the early part of his life, previous to coming to West Simsbury, was a seaman. His oldest son John resided at or near the place now occupied by Martin Moses. Mr. Taylor died of the small-pox; he was quite sure that he had had it in the West Indies; but when his son John's children had it, and seeing how hard it went with them, he was led to believe that he might be mistaken with regard to himself, and was accordingly inocculated with the small-pox and died, and was buried on the hill north-west of the house of Elijah Whiting.

Parents.	Born. Died. Age.	
William Taylor,	1777.	
Ruth Higgins,	1813.	

Children.	Born. Died. Age.	
———.		Married Asa Wilcox.
William, Jun,,	1757, 1835, 78.	Married Abigail Case.
Ozias,	1814.	Married Amelia Humphrey.
Ruth.		
David,	1840.	Married 1st Lucina Roberts; 2d, Marlow Johnson.
Isaiah,	1767, 1811, 43.	Married Zilpah Case.

ENSIGN ISAAC TULLER was an early settler in West Simsbury. He removed from the Old Parish about 1749. He was the third son of Sarah Woodford, who died in 1797, aged 100 years. He resided on the place that was afterward occupied by his son Rufus, and is now (1855) the property of Augustus H. Carrier.

There were eleven children in this family, three sons and eight daughters, all of whom lived to adult years, and ten of them had children.

Parents.	Born. Died. Age.	
Isaac Tuller,	1720, 1806, 86.	Married 1746.
Phebe Case,	1728, 1799, 71.	Daughter of James Case.

Children.	Born. Died. Age.	
Phebe,	1747, 1776, 29.	Married James Case, son of Josiah Case.
Isaac, Jun.,	1749, 1776, 28.	Died in the army at Bergen, N. J.

Deliverance,	1751, 1805, 54.	Married Isaac Wilcox.
Ruth,	1755, 1818, 63.	Married Frederick Humphrey.
Esther,	1757, 1851. 94.	Married Elijah Hill.
Lois,	1759, 1797, 37.	Married James Lawrence.
Sarah,	1761, 1812, 51.	Married Ozias Northway.
Aseneth,	1763, 1815, 52.	Married Jonathan Merrell.
Amasa,	1765, 1792, 27.	Married Sylvia Case.
Rufus,*	1767.	Married Matilda Case.
Chloe,	1770, 1845, 75.	Married Timothy Cadwell.

HISTORICAL SKETCHES OF THE ANCESTRY OF THE WILCOX FAMILIES IN SIMSBURY, CANTON. &c.

SAMUEL WILCOX, (then spelt Wilcoxson,) was the ancestor of all those that bear the name of Wilcox in this vicinity. He was an early settler in Simsbury, but the exact time is not known. It appears that he resided at Meadow Plain, and as Avon, adjoining to Simsbury, had at its early existence, some families of that name, it is probable that they sprung from this early stock through Samuel, 2d, the oldest son of the first Samuel. He had three sons, viz., Samuel, 2d, William and Joseph. It is not known that any of the descendants of the second Samuel ever settled in West Simsbury. Samuel, 2d, had sons, Joseph, born 1701; Ephraim, born 1707, and probably others. William, son of the first Samuel, had sons, John, William, 2d, known by the title of Dea. William, Amos and Azariah. Dea. William had sons, William, 3d, or Lieut. William who settled in West Simsbury. (See *History of Lieut. William Wilcox.*) Amos, another brother of Dea. William, had Amos, 2d, called Col. Amos, three brothers and five sisters; none of them became residents of this town. Azariah had sons, Elisha, 1st, Aaron, and others. Elisha was father of the late Elisha, 2d, and Col. Azariah, and was the ancestor of Harvey and Chester

*The oldest person now (1856) living in Canton, being in his 89th year.

and their sisters. Joseph, 1st, the third son of Samuel, 1st, born 1674, was the father of the Joseph Wilcox, race in Canton. (See *History of Joseph Wilcox 1st, and 2d.*) There was raised up in the north-east part of Simsbury or Granby, Joseph Wilcox, Esq., who was son to the second Samuel; this Joseph was justice of the peace, representative, &c., for some twenty years, subsequent to 1738, who is supposed to be father of Joseph and Hosea Wilcox, of Norfolk, who were old men at Norfolk in 1800, but were never inhabitants of Canton. Joseph, 1st, was the father of Joseph Jun., Hezekiah, Nathaniel, Ezra, 1st, or Sen., and sisters.

There was an Ephraim Wilcox, appeared in West Simsbury about 1746. He might be a brother of Esquire Joseph, but this is uncertain. Ephraim, aforementioned, married the widow of Thomas Bidwell, Sen., and was the father of Philander, Martin, Asa and Jehiel. (See *History of Philander Wilcox and Brothers.*)

JOSEPH WILCOX, SEN., was son of the first Samuel Wilcox, (then spelt Wilcoxson.) He came from the Old Parish to reside among his sons and spend the latter part of his days with them; when he came to West Simsbury is not definitely known.

Parents.	Born.	Died.	Age.	
Joseph Wilcox, Sen.,	1674,	1770.	96.	Married 1703.
Abigail Thrall,		17—.		Daughter of Timothy Thrall.

Children, as far as known.	Born.	Died.	Age.	
Joseph, Jun.,	1706,	1759,	53.	Married Elizabeth Humphrey, 1735.
Sarah,	1712.			
Hezekiah,	1713,	1789,	75.	
Nathaniel, } Twins,	1719,	1791,	72.	A cripple; married Rachel Moses.
Mary, } Twins,	1719,	1756,	37.	Married Samuel Humphrey, 3d, 1731.
Ezra,	1723,	1786,	63.	Married Mary Humphrey.

JOSEPH WILCOX, JUN., with his wife, came to West Simsbury about the year 1738. He lived on the place which was afterward owned by his nephew, Ezra Wilcox, Jun., nearly opposite the present mouth of Cherries brook. He was called a man of uncommon strength and resolution. He was killed instantly by a fall from a scaffold in his barn, A. D. 1759. He was donor of the land for the South-burying ground.

Parents.	Born. Died. Age.	
Joseph Wilcox, Jun.,	1706, 1759, 53.	Married 1735.
Elizabeth Humphrey,		Daughter of Samuel Humphrey.

NATHANIEL WILCOX, son of Joseph, Sen., with his wife, came to West Simsbury about the year 1743. He settled on land around the site of the old first bridge, on Farmington river. His house stood at the foot of the hill on the west side of the river, west of the old bridge place. The bridge then stood some twenty rods south of the present bridge, and west of the house of Harlow Case. The old road went up the steep hill west of his house; some remains of it are still to be seen.

Parents.	Born. Died. Age.	
Nathaniel Wilcox,	1719, 1791, 72.	Married 1743.
Rachel Moses,	1807.	

Children.	Born. Died. Age.	
Nathaniel, Jun.,	1776.	Died in the army.
Joseph,	1776.	Died a prisoner.
Rachel.		Married Joseph Hawkins.
Seth,	1787.	His widow married Dr. Nathaniel Hooker.
Sarah.		Married 1st, —— Carter; 2d, —— Monger.
Temperance.		Married Joseph Snath.
Son.		Died at the house of Elisha Cornish, Simsbury.

Lieut. WILLIAM WILCOX, son of Dea. William Wilcox, of Simsbury, Meadow Plain, with his wife, whose maiden mame was Lucy Case, daughter of John Case, 3d, came to West Simsbury about the year 1750. He settled on land now belonging to Ruggles Case, Esq. They had thirteen children including three who died in infancy or childhood.

Parents.	Born.	Died.	Age.
William Wilcox,	1727,	1775,	48.
Lucy Case,	1732,	1805,	73.

Children.	Born.	Died.	Age.	
Lucy,				Married Moses Case.
Charles,				Married 1st, Thankful Mills; 2d, Abigail Case.
William, Jun.,	1756,	1827,	71.	Married 1st, Mercy Case, 2d, Mrs. Anna Moses.
Mary.				Married Eliphalet Curtis, Jun.
Jedediah,	1763,	1818,	55.	Married Sarah Case.
Thankful,	1761.			Married Zimri Barber.
Imri,	1765,	1807,	42.	Married Lucretia Hayes.
Lovisa,	1767.			Married Dudley Mills.
Dan,	1773,	1833,	61.	Married Esther Merrett.
Sterling,	1774,	1823,	48.	Married Sophia Denslow.

Capt. CHARLES WILCOX, son of Lieut. William, married 1771, for his first wife, Thanks Mills, daughter of Dea. Joseph Mills. They had three little sons, viz., Philemon, born, 1772; Charles born 1774, and Billy, born 1775. These three with their mother, all died between the 28th of August and the 12th of September, 1776, of the malignant dysentery, a disease that raged at that time in the army, and among the citizens at home, through a great portion of the northern states.

The husband and father of the deceased ones subsequently married Abigail, daughter of Capt. Zacheus Case. They were the parents of Abigail, Thanks, Achsah and Philemon; but another dreadful stroke awaited them, for in September, 1787, Achsah, aged 3 years, and Philemon aged 10 months, died of the dreadful disease called croup or rattles in the throat. They died on the 27th of September, 1787, but fifteen minutes apart and were both buried in one coffin. They afterward had (as it is understood) four children.

Col. WILLIAM WILCOX, the fourth of the name in direct succession, and son of Lieut. William and Mrs. Lucy Wilcox. For his first wife he married Mercy, daughter of Capt. Zacheus Case, and for his second, Anna, widow of Lieut. Daniel Moses, whose maiden name was Anna Edgerton. He resided on the premises, and erected the house now owned by his son Orville Wilcox, in the North school-district,

Parents.	Born.	Died.	Age.	
William Wilcox,	1758,	1827,	69.	Married December 22d, 1779.
1st wife, Mercy Case,	1761,	1809,	48.	
2d wife, Anna Edgerton,	1775,	1846,	71.	

Children.	Born.	Died.	Age.	
Mercy,	1780,	1806,	26.	
William, Jun.,	1782.			Married 1st, Roxy McFarland; 2d, Mercy Rice.
Zacheus,	1785,	1826,	41.	Married Temperance Case.
Alanson,	1787,	1849,	62.	Married Cyrene Johnson.
Orville,	1792.			Married widow of Chester Giddings.
Celestia,	1794.			
Garmon,	1796.			Married Louisa C. Wright.
Rodman,	1789,	1837,	47.	Married Rosanna Gwin.
Imri,	1798,	1835,	37.	Died single.
Loyal,	1800.			Married Almira Reed.
Philena,	1802,	1854,	52.	Married Lucius Brooks.
Mariah,	1812.			Married Marvin Case.

COL. AZARIAH WILCOX, son of Elisha Wilcox, Sen., and grandson of Azariah Wilcox, 1st. He resided on the place now owned by Sidney S. Sexton, in the Farms school-district. He married a daughter of Benajah Humphrey, Jun.

Parents.	Born.	Died.	Age.
Azariah Wilcox,		1814,	58.
Hepzibeth Humphrey.			

Children.	Born.	Died.	Age.	
Benajah, about	1778.			
Caroline.				
Chloe.				
Tammy Lovet,	1793.			
Azariah Jay,	1795,	1812,	18.	Drowned at Tariffville.
Hepzibeth,				Married Henry Harrington.

SERG. EZRA WILCOX, SEN., with his wife Mary, daughter of Samuel Humphrey, 2d, removed from the Old Parish to West Simsbury about A. D. 1743, His place of residence was on the west side of the river, opposite the mouth of Cherries brook. He married for his second wife, Rhoda, widow of Philip Harris.

Parents.	Born.	Died.	Age.
Ezra Wilcox,	1723,	1786,	63.
Mary Humphrey,		1756.	

Children.	Born.	Died.	Age.	
Ezra, Jun.,	1746,	1807,	61.	Married Rosanna Case.
Rachel, } twins,	1748.			
Mary, }		1756,	8.	
Elizabeth,	1750.			Married Joseph Mabison, of New Canaan, N. Y.
Isaac,	1753.			Married Deliverance Tuller.
Lucy,	1754.			Married John Nearing.
Phebe,	1756,			Married William Noble.
Giles,	1759,	1777,	18.	Died single.

John.	Removed to the region of Whitestown, N. Y., 1791.
Hezekiah.	Removed to the region of Whitestown, N. Y., 1791.
Rhoda.	Married Obadiah Taylor.
Zeruiah,	Married Samuel Humphrey, Jun., or 5th.

EZRA WILCOX, Jun., son of Ezra Wilcox and Mary Humphrey. He married Rosanna, daughter of Dea. Abraham and Mrs. Rachel Case. He resided on the premises owned and occupied by his uncle, Joseph Wilcox, Jun., e- ceased, near the confluence of the turnpike and the river road.

Parents.	Born. Died. Age.	
Ezra Wilcox, Jun., or 2d,	1746, 1807, 61.	
Rosanna Case,	1746, 1807, 61.	Both were born and both died the same year.

Children.	Born. Died. Age.	
Abraham,	1769, 1815, 46.	Married Arabella Dyer.
Faith,	1771.	Married Jesse Moory.
Alexander,	1773.	Married ——— Nearing.
Allen,	1775, 1830, 55.	Married Chloe Woodford.
Eunice,	1776.	Married Giles Woodford.
Clarissa,	1779.	Married James Moses.
Mary,	1781.	
Gad,	1783.	Died single.
Edmund,	1788.	Still lives single, (1856.)

ISAAC WILCOX, second son of Ezra Wilcox, Sen., married Deliverance, daughter of Ensign Isaac Tuller. He resided on the premises and erected the dwelling-house now owned by Zenas and Daniel Dyer. In the year 1801, he removed to Pompey, State of New York.

Parents.	Born. Died. Age.	
Isaac Wilcox,	1753.	
Deliverance Tuller,	1751, 1805, 54.	

Children.	Born. Died. Age.	
Isaac, Jun.		Married Margaret Tooly.
Starling.		

CAPT. DANIEL WILCOX. He married Lydia, daughter of Samuel Humphrey, 2d, 1737. He resided on the place now occupied by Julius Case about the year 1750. He lost his property by being bound for the owners of the old forge, which was swept away by a flood from its place, on the north-east side of the river, above the old school-house place. They had no children.

Parents.	Born. Died. Age.
Daniel Wilcox.	
Lydia Humphrey,	1775.

COL. AMOS WILCOX, with his wife, Hannah Hoskins, came from the Old Parish and settled on land now belonging to Capt. Jerry Wilcox, his grandson, about the year 1752. They had nine children, six sons and three daughters; seven of them settled in family state and raised up families.

Parents.	Born. Died. Age.	
Amos Wilcox,	1726, 1785, 59.	Married 1749.
Hannah Hoskins,	1726, 1779, 53.	

Children.	Born. Died. Age.	
Amos, Jun.,	1750, 1844, 94.	Married Annah Case.
Hannah,	1755, 1801, 46.	First wife of Ezra Adams, Esq.
David,	1753.	Married Mary Cornish.
Roger,	1752, 1825, 73.	Married Elizabeth Case.

Phebe,	1758, 1828, 70.	Married Rev. Seth Sage: he died 1822.
Zelek,	1763, 1807, 45.	
Joel, } twins,	1765. 1826, 61.	
Betsy, } twins,	1765. 1810, 45.	First wife of William Merrell.
Robert,	1767, 1847, 79.	Married Climena Mills.

AMOS WILCOX, JUN., son of Amos Wilcox, Sen. He with his wife Annah, daughter of Capt. Josiah Case, commenced family state about 1772. He resided on the premises now owned by Salmon Matson, in the north-east corner of the town.

Parents.	Born. Died. Age.
Amos Wilcox, Jun.,	1750. 1844, 94.
Annah Case,	1750, 1833, 83.

Children.	Born. Died. Age.	
Annah, 2d,	1773.	
Cherissa,	1775.	Married Gad Curtis.
Amos, 3d,	1777.	Married ——— Lattimer.
Buckland,	1848.	
Ruth.		Married Timothy Graham.
Betsy,		Married Jedadiah Wilcox.
Jeptha.		
Orren.		
Willys.		

EPHRAIM WILCOX, married Ruhamah, widow of Thomas Bidwell, Sen., and resided on the premises left by said Thomas, for a number of years They had four sons, viz., Philander, Jehiel, Asa, Martin, and one daughter, Chloe, who married Elijah Humphrey.

PHILANDER WILCOX settled on the farm previously owned by William Payne. He, for his first wife, married Abigail Fuller; she died 1785, leaving two daughters. He for his second wife, married Mercia Moses, by whom he had two more daughters; one of them married Carmi Case; the other married Salmon Barber. He removed in 1803, to Barkhamsted Hollow, where he resided through life and died in 1813. His widow survived him some years and died in Barkhamsted.

JEHIEL WILCOX, brother to Philander, married a daughter of Saunders Moore, of Granby. He resided on the farm previously owned by John Taylor, between his brothers Philander and Asa, which is now the residence of Martin Moses. He removed to Barkhamsted about the year ——, where he resided till about 1808, when he removed to the State of Ohio, where he spent the remainder of his life, and died a few years since, aged 85.

ASA WILCOX, another brother, resided on the farm afterward owned by Dea. Alvin Humphrey. He married a daughter of William, Sen., and Ruth Taylor. They had children, Prudence, Billy, Asa, and others.

GAMALIEL WARD and SIMEON WARD. They settled in 1745, on the farm, now the west part of the premises of Eliphalet Case. Their house stood on the west side of Cherries brook, the west side of the road, a few rods north of the bridge. It is not in the power of the writer to tell, whether they two were brothers or father and son.

Parents.	Born. Died. Age.	
Gamaliel Ward,	1694, 1774, 80.	
Elizabeth Simons.		
Simeon Ward,	1780.	

Children.	Born. Died. Age.	
Betsy,	1740, 1825, 85.	Married Amos Case, Jun.
Mindwell.		Married James McNall.
Anna,		Married Isaac Messenger, Jun.
James,	1754, 1777, 23.	Died of small-pox.
Infant.	1762.	

URIAH WHITNEY, with his wife, Miss —— Hart, of Avon, resided in the Farms school-district. Among their children were Samuel and Lucy, and others not known to the writer. He lived on the farm subsequently owned by Noble Phelps. The buildings then stood on the east side of the highway, northeasterly from the dwelling house of the late said Noble Phelps, deceased; in the year 1801, he removed to Granville, Mass. Nothing further is known of his or his family's history.

[NOTE. The following genealogical notes of the sons of Dea. Hosea Case were not received in time for insertion in their proper alphabetical order.]

HOSEA CASE, JUN., first son of Dea. Hosea Case. He married for his first wife, Rhoda, daughter of Amos Case, Sen., and for his second, Sarah, daughter of Solomon Buel, Sen. He commenced his farming operation in the town of Norfolk; from there he removed back to West Simsbury and settled on the place now owned by Alvin Bacon. He afterward moved on to the farm now owned by Giles A. Sisson, where he spent the remainder of his life.

Parents.	Born.	Died.	Age.	
Hosea Case, Oct.	6, 1756,	1834,	78.	
Rhoda Case, April	20, 1757,	1786,	29.	
Sarah Buel,	1760,	1838,	78.	Married A. D. 1787.

Child.	Born.	Died.	Age.	
Rhoda,	1780,	1847,	67.	Married Loin Humphrey.

ASA CASE, SEN., second son of Dea. Hosea Case, married for his first wife, Lois, daughter of Solomon Dill; for his second, Thede, widow of Benajah Humphrey, and daughter of Capt. Zacheus Case. He lived on the place now owned by his youngest son, Milton Case.

Parents.	Born.	Died.	Age.	
Asa Case,	1758,	1837,	79.	Married January 28th, 1781.
Lois Dill,	1759,	1812,	53.	
Thede Humphrey,	1766,	1851,	85.	

Children.	Born.	Died.	Age.	
Lois, } twins,	Oct. 1782,	1783.		
Lorinda, } twins,	Oct. 1782,	1787.		
Asa, Jun., Dec.	1, 1786.			Married Hepzibah Buel.
Dosa, March	7, 1788.			Married Tirza Case.
Bera, July	22, 1790.			Married Sarah Humphrey.

Daughter,	May	25, 1793, 1793.	
Hosea,	June	13, 1794, 1827, 33.	Married 1st, Thede M. Humphrey; 2d, Charlotte Mills.
Lois,	Dec.	23, 1796, 1846, 50.	Married Solomon V. Case.
Lorinda,	March	24, 1799, 1833, 34.	Married Orson Reed.
Milton.	Feb.	19, 1801.	Married Eunice Reed.

TITUS CASE, fourth son of Dea. Hosea Case. He married for his first wife, Rebecca Eggleston; second wife, Phebe Tuttle. He commenced his family state on the East Hill, on the place now occuped by Reuben S. Hull. The last years of his life he lived about fifty rods south of the meeting-house, Canton center.

Parents.	Born. Died. Age.	
Titus Case,	1768, 1845, 76.	Married January 28th, 1790.
Rebecca Eggleston.		
Phebe Tuttle.		

Children.		Born. Died. Age.	
Rebecca,	Nov.	14, 1790.	Married John Garrett.
Sarah,	May	6, 1793.	Married Calvin Case.
Titus S.	April	23, 1796, 1835, 39.	Married Terrissa Humphrey.
Francis H.	Oct.	1, 1797.	Married Lucinda Case.
Mary,	April	20, 1800. 1808, 8.	
Polly,	April	23, 1809.	Married Calvin Case, Jun.

CHAPTER

ON THE

Black Citizens of West Simsbury.

JAMES BALTIMORE, known as Jim Balt, was an inhabitant of this town as early or earlier than 1774. He resided with or near Capt. Dudley Case, in the part of New Hartford that is now Canton. His first wife died as early as 1780, and left two children, viz., Polly, born 1775, and Sam, born 1778. Sam remained with Capt. Dud (so called) for nearly thirty years, and was indulged with greater privileges and liberties than commonly fall to the lot of colored people in families of wealth and standing. He appeared to talk as though he had a good share of influence and direction in the common departments of business, and was known to say that Capt. Dud, should never come to want while he lived. The sister, Poll, fared harder in the world, and saw much trouble and ill-usage. They both left this part of the country many years ago. James, the father, for second wife, married Susannah, daughter of Col. London Wallace. (Negroes received and valued military and civil titles of honor highly.) He was set up on the east end of the farm of Charles and Benajah Humphrey, south-east of the house of Bera Case. They had a number of children; part of them died in infancy and childhood. While the family remained in their tenement, it was the place of resort for colored people, both relatives and others, which is generally the case where the colored people have a shelter, a family, and something to live on for the present.

LONDON CHESTER, (called *Governor*, as it was understood that he had held that office among the Wethersfield negroes.) He was through the prime of life, the servant of Col. John Chester, the elder. It is not known at what period of time he received his freedom. He had a wife named Betty, and during the last years of her life he resided at the place now called Indian Hill, on the premises now owned by the Messrs. Pike. His wife died in 1787, and he after that time became dependent on the public for support. It appears from his own statements that he came from Africa quite young, as he spoke better English than was common for that race. One incident he used to relate, would show that he came to this country young. He said that in the early part of his life with Master Chester, he saw one morning what he thought to be a very pretty puppy; he accordingly seized him with a view to play with him, but the skunk soon convinced him that he was playing with the wrong animal. From that story originated the name of "Wethersfield puppy." He died near the close of the last century, aged about 80 years, a pauper supported by New Hartford.

CHARLES PRINCE married Tabitha Quamino; he had been several years in the employ of Capt. Dudley Case, and was viewed by the family and the people of the neighborhood, as an honest, industrious and meritorious citizen, and still more, he and his wife were called worthy members of the church. He died of consumption, A. D. 1828, and the process had already begun whereby he was wronged out of the small pittance of landed estate which his deceased patron had given him years before, but had not executed the deed; from that period the family appeared to sink under their misfortunes. Some died, some left the town, and very little is known respecting the circumstances of the survivors if any yet remaim.

SIMON FLETCHER, known as Lieut. Simon, erected a house, and lived in it on the land of Capt. Dudley Case. It should be borne in mind that Capt. Case, with his first wife Susanna, were reputed kind guardians of the blacks, and helpers of the indigent whites who lived on his premises or in the neighborhood. Simon's house stood by the brook, at the foot of the hill on the road leading to Harvey Mills residence. The name of his wife is not known, neither the number of his children, but among his children was Julius, who had his skull broken in by the kick of a horse; Julius was born about 1775. The family disappeared from this part as early as 1795. Simon was what is called a second or third rate fiddler, and the same may be said of a great share of the men of color of those times. On the east confines of New Hartford, and on the north-west part of Old Simsbury, called Negrotown, were many blacks, and among them a good number of fiddlers. It was also observable, that wherever there was a colored family that possessed in good measure the comforts of life, there were sure to be plenty of hangers on.

CÆSAR WILCOX was probably brought from Africa after he had arrived to adult years. He through life, spoke very broken English. He, or his services, were called the property of Joseph Wilcox, 2d, or Jun. When his master was found dead by his fall in the barn in 1759, Cæsar was the one who first discovered him ; he went into the house to inform his mistress, but so broken was his language; that it required a long time with the help of signs, before he could make her understand what he wanted to communicate to her. He was afterward sold into the State of New York, where he remained till after the death of his master. The writer of this article once heard him say that he dug his second master's grave. It was currently reported that while living in the State of New York, he married or cohabited with a woman of his race, and they had some children. He in some way left his New York residence and returned to Connecticut; the time not definitely known, but probably as late as 1780, after which he lived in an unsettled state, according as he found friends or employers; sometimes faring middling well, and sometimes very poor. When Canton was incorporated in 1806, he by agreement was taken by Old Simsbury, who supported him during the last years of his life. He died in 1812, quite aged, having seen enough of this world's kindness toward worn out blacks.

There have been several colored persons who have resided a few years in Canton, but not in family state at so early a period as what this work is treating of. This general remark is true with respect to Canton, as with other towns, and even with Connecticut, viz., that the colored race have strangely dwindled away, and in great measure disappeared within the last sixty-five years, and no one can tell what has become of them. There were, at different periods of time, between 1750 and 1776, some four or five negroes held as servants. Some of them had died, and those that remained were voluntarily released.

SKETCH OF THE

First Ecclesiastical Society of West Simsbury,

NOW CANTON.

About the year 1741, the people of West Simsbury began to hold religious meetings on the Sabbath, in private houses. From 1747 to 1750, two preachers, Rev. Adonijah Bidwell and Rev. Timothy Pitkin, were employed to preach, each for a short time. This section of the town was constituted a distinct parish by an act of the General Assembly, May, 1750. The Congregational church was organized, it is supposed, about the same time. The same year, Rev. Evander Morrison, who was from Scotland, was installed first pastor of the church. For some cause, Mr. Morrison was dismissed about eleven months after his installation. The next pastor was Rev. Gideon Mills, who was installed in 1759, and continued pastor of the church thirteen years. The third pastor was Rev. Seth Sage, installed 1774, and dismissed 1778. Rev. Jeremiah Hallock was the fourth pastor of the church. He was ordained October 26th, 1785, and continued pastor till his death in June, 1826, a period of about forty-one years. Rev. Jairus Burt; the present pastor, was ordained December 20th, 1826.

The first meeting-house was built in 1763, and was occupied by the society fifty-one years, having been taken down in 1814. A new house erected on the same spot, (now Canton Center,) was dedicated January 5th, 1815. (See *Phelps' History of Simsbury, Granby and Canton.*)

NOTABLE EVENTS.

And remarkable seasons which occurred at different periods, and were of public notoriety at the time of their happening, and had an important bearing on many individuals, and in some instances on the whole population of the then inhabitants of the society of West Simsbury, (now Canton.)

1755.—The French War which existed in former years at different periods, became more operative and distressing to New England and the other northern States. Certain youngerly men were called into the English army; some of them lost their lives.

1762.—Was the time of the unfortunate expedition against Havannah; several young men went in a company which was raised principally, in the then town of Simsbury, under the command of Capt. Noah Humphrey. Among the soldiers of that company were Dudley Miller, and Jonathan Barber, both of whom died. Theophilus Humphrey went and lived to return.

1763.—Was memorable for the peace between England and France.

1775.—Memorable for the commencement of the Revolutionary War, which called many men into the army in the vicinity of Boston.

1776.—Memorable for the declaration of American independence; the many disasters that befel the American army, both by defeat and by mortal sickness, which prevailed among the officers and soldiers in the army, and spread among the citizens at home in the summer and autumn, and sent death and mourning into many families, and almost entirely destroyed some, that a few weeks before were prosperous and healthful.

1777.—Was memorable to Canton, by the breaking out of the small-pox among the people; some six to ten died, and others were brought, as it were, to death's door. Soldiers returning from the war, brought the disease and gave it to their famiiies and friends. The sufferings and privations of the people were great; among many other things, the want of laborers to raise and harvest the crops, necessary for the sustenence of life to man and beast. It was a well-authenticated fact at the time and afterward, that many females belonging to respectable families, from the necessity of the case, voluntarily performed manual labor on the farms, with the hoe, the manure fork, the hay fork and the sickle, and other farming tools commonly used by farmers and their sons. It would surely be a sight worth looking at for the young females at the present day, if they could see their grandmothers performing that labor which was laid upon them for the helps of their families and their country.

1778.—The latter part of this year and the beginning of 1779, was memorable for much sickness in North Canton; the disease was then called the long fever.

1779.—Memorable for a very early and forward spring. It passed as a well-attested fact by credible men, that apple trees were in full blossom on the 15th of April; but there afterward came a severe and cutting frost that destroyed all the fruit.

1779--80.—This winter was remarkably severe and long, attended with excessive deep snows, which occasioned great hardships and sufferings in various ways to man and beast.

1780.—Was noted for the dark day that occurred May 19th. It was probably occasioned by an accumulation of thick and dense masses of vapor and smoke.

1781.—Was memorable for the burning of New London and the inhuman butchery of the garrison at fort Griswold, on Groton hill; but Connecticut was soon cheered with the joyful news of the capture of Lord Cornwallis, which put a brighter appearance on the prospects of America.

1783.—Was blessed and the country with it, by bringing about peace between England and the United States; and the return home of officers and soldiers from the army. This year was also noted for the great revival of religion which commenced early in the summer and continued into the year 1784. There were a goodly number then added to the visible Church, who very generally through life, were an honor to the blessed cause which they professed, and so lived and died as to obtain a good report. The fruits of that revival have all been gathered in. Mr. Edmund Mills, nephew of the Rev. Gideon Mills, the former minister, was the preacher for a number of months, assisted by Messrs. Robins, Gillett, Mills, Miller, Smalley, and others, who were providentially sent there to preach and attend religious meetings.

1785.—Was blessed by the ministerial labors and settlement of the Rev. Mr. Hallock, whose pious and useful labors with us continued more than forty years.

1786.—Was memorable for the appearance of the insect called the Hessian fly. It was among other events noted for an extreme high and destructive flood in October.

1787.—Memorable by the promulgation of the new Constitution of the United States. Some in Simsbury liked it, while others hated it. The town of Simsbury instructed their two delegates, Gen. Noah Phelps, and Esquire Daniel Humphrey, to oppose its adoption by the State, and they obeyed their instructions, though Esquire Humphrey said it was against his personal inclination, but it was adopted in the State Constitution in January, 1788.

1788.—Was a wet, cold unfruitful summer; grain of all kinds very poor. A very destructive wind or hurricane in August, which prostrated the poor standing corn, made great destruction in the groves of wood, injured many buildings, and entirely destroyed some.

1789.—Was a time of uncommon scarcity for bread, the staff of life, and almost a famine was occasioned by the previous unfruitful year. Many families who were termed good livers, and of middling property, lived on bran bread, while others ordered their rye ground without bolting, and in other respects, lived on food to correspond with it, while many were much troubled to obtain that coarse fare, for labor or money. In a word, it was a time of great scarcity and extreme suffering among the people, till the last of July, when the rye went to the grist mill, very soon from the hands of the reapers. In the spring of this year, blossoms and vegetation generally were backward, but the summer was fruitful. In October, appeared among us and through this region of country, the epidemic called influenza. It proved destructive to many, especially to the aged and infirm. It appeared again in April and May, 1790, with similar effect.

1793.—Was a year of much sickness among children and youth; the disease was canker rash or scarlet fever, which sent sorrow and mourning into many families.

1794.—The spring was uncommonly early and forward; apple blossoms were seen as early as the 22d of April, vegetation progressed rapidly, blossoms fell off, and were followed by the young fruit, but on the night of the 17th of May, there came a destructive frost that killed fruit and vegetation, which was so forward that even rye was killed on some low land, and garden productions destroyed, all that could be hurt by the frost.

1795.—Was termed a favorable year for farmers; English grain, corn, and grass uncommonly good; grain and live stock commanding a high price. But the seeds were germinating whereby in 1796, the American commerce was seriously annoyed, both by England and France, which annoyance continued till 1800. The Jay treaty settled the matter as it respected England, but it raised the jealousy of France in 1796, which eventuated in French depredations on American commerce, which lasted till the conclusion of the Ellsworth treaty in 1800. During the four years previous to 1800, there were honorable politicians, who by looking through different glasses, saw the position of the different parties, and in this period the two great parties called Federalists and Democrats arose, and entered the political field in violent combat against each other, both of them claiming the honor of following the political opinions, and walking in the footsteps of the great Father of his country—Washington. This party strife has passed through different shapes, assumed various names and enlisted and paid different partisans, for more than sixty years; but enough of these remarks. The great political campaign of 1800, resulted in a change of men and measures, as respected the national government; and there have been the ins and the outs, as respected power, at all periods, in the country's history.

1798.—Was memorable by a great and powerful work of the Holy Spirit, in awakening and hopefully converting many stout-hearted sinners, and among them some who had fortified themselves in infidelity. The reformation appeared to be notable, and was visible through their after lives. See the notice of that revival as published in the Connecticut Evangelical Magazine, for December, 1800.

1801.—March was rendered memorable by the inauguration of President Jefferson in the chair of state. A notable event soon after followed, viz., the Jefferson flood, an event of great notoriety. It far surpassed anything of the kind within the memory of the oldest of the Fathers, and most of the high water marks yet remain unsurpassed for the last fifty-five years. It carried off the grist and saw mill belonging to Moses & Cleveland, (situated west of the house of Marvin Case,) and in it a boy and girl belonging to Mr. Josiah Atkins; the girl was saved but the boy perished, aged 16 years. His body was found in the meadows more than a mile below the mill.

The winters of 1801 and 1802 were uncommonly mild and open; but the winter of 1803-4; was remarkable in the opposite extreme. The winter commenced in earnest on the 24th of December, and continued with increasing severity, and without material mitigation, until near the last of March. The snows were frequent, and very deep on a level, and were by the wind whirled into drifts of uncommon depth, so that most of the roads except the most public, and constant traveled ones, were wholly forsaken and untraveled for several weeks. There were deep snow-drifts, even in some sunshining places till near the last days of May. It was at that time thought to surpass any winter that had been since 1780.

1805.—Was in some respects notable for good to Canton in religious concerns. There were appearances of an awakening in June At that time the vegetable world was to appearance, threatened with a severe drouth, especially the Indian corn. On the last sabbath in July, Mr. Hallock appointed a day of humiliation and prayer for the church and people, on the following Wednesday, taking into considtion the low state of religion, and the dependence of the people on the great Giver of all good. The day came and was observed by the religious community, with some degree of sincerity. But during the afternoon of that day the people were met by a plentiful supply of temporal rain, and an apparent increase of spiritual blessings. The weeks that followed were weeks of fruitfulness. The religious part of the community were wont to speak of that favor as a kind interposition of a merciful God.

1806.—Was memorable for the incorporation of the town of Canton. With respect to the season, a severe drouth commenced in June and lasted till September. It killed the turf in many of the upland mow lots, but the summer of 1807, was so extremely wet and growing, as to restore the ground to its wonted greenness.

1808.—Was memorable to Canton by the malady called the spotted fever, which in April, May and June, sent death, and sorrow, and mourning, into many of our dwellings.

1809--10.—The winter of 1809--10, was noted as a remarkable open winter. It was literally true that people might, as respected the state of the ground, have plowed every month in the winter.

1810.—Was very memorable for the sudden change from warm to cold, which happened on the 18th of January. The afternoon of that day was uncommonly mild and even warm for the season, but before eleven o'clock that night, the cold was intense, and the wind blowing a hurricane. The public journals of that period told of many strange appearances; of freezing high wind, upon agitated, freezing water. Many buildings were blown down, and many trees prostrated. The cold continued violent for three succeeding days; then the sudden changes from one extreme of cold or heat to the other, went on as it had done before.

1812.—Was memorable by the breaking out of the war between America and England, which raged with great violence for nearly three years. Different politicians of the different beligerent nations, did, for the time being, express their different views respecting the call for the war, but both nations were extremely glad to be rid of it soon as possible.

1814.—Was memorable to the Congregational church and society of Canton. The meeting-house having become too small for the congregation, and also dilapidated, it was almost unanimously agreed by the society to build a new and commodious house, provided the means could be raised by subscription to defray the expense. The papers were circulated, and the people mostly throughout the entire town, subscribed more or less, and many of the society very liberally, for the object. The necessary funds being raised, the society voted to build on the old site, and with great unanimity and strength removed the old house, reduced the hill on which it stood, and made a dry and pleasant site for the new house. The work of collecting materials for building was soon commenced, at which point Mr. Orange Case, one of the most enterprising and valuable members of the church and society was instantly killed by the falling of a tree, which tree was designed for a part of the frame of the new house. This solemn and unexpected event cast a gloom over the community that was not soon forgotten. But not withstanding this afflictive dispensation, the Lord gave the people strength and a united heart to go forward and build the house for his worship. The summer season was remarkable for the frequent and powerful showers, accompanied with unusual thunder and lightning, rendering the earth less productive than usual, yet there was a competency for the wants of the people.

1816.—Was remarkable for a cold summer, so much so that the effects of frost were visible in every month except August, during the season. The Indian corn was almost entirely cut off, and the small portion that remained was materially injured. The rye harvest, though threatened by the frosts, was wonderfully preserved and remarkably good, furnishing for the people beyond their most sanguine expectations, the staff of life.

1821.—Was a year of unusual interest on account of a revival of religion, by which the church was strengthened by numbers and graces.

1826.—Was remarkable for the barrenness of the fore part of the summer, which caused a scarcity of food in the pastures, and a short crop of hay for the cattle, by means of which the price of stock was extremely depressed. About the last of August came one of the most powerful rains ever known in this vicinity, and occasioned one of the greatest freshets ever known by the oldest inhabitants, sweeping away mills, bridges, fences and roads, in a manner almost unparalleled. The rain fell principally between the hours of 10 A. M. and 1 P. M.

The latter part of the season was favorable for the products of the earth, which were brought to maturity and furnished the means of subsistance for man and beast. This year was memorable also, on account of the death of Rev. Jeremiah Hallock, the faithful and devoted pastor of the church. The important and interesting relation that had long existed between him and his people was dissolved by his death on the 23d day of June, 1826. His death occasioned the most intense feeling and deep interest, and spread an almost impenetrable cloud over the community; yet his pious and devoted life, and his peaceful death, carried the conviction to every reflecting mind, that he had exchanged this world of toil, and care, and pain, for that better and brighter world above.

His amiable and beloved consort closed her connection with earthly scenes on the 3d day of November, 1826. She was a bright example of industry, economy and piety, always ready to do all in her power to relieve the sick and suffering, and promote the spiritual and temporal welfare of the people. "The heart of her husband did safely trust in her, and her children did rise up and call her blessed."

Soon after the death of Mr. Hallock, the interesting and important question began to be raised, Where shall we go, and whom shall we find to fill the place made vacant by his death?

The committee of the church and society were directed to Mr. Jairus Burt, a licentiate then preaching in Colerain, Mass. He was accordingly invited to supply the pulpit for a time, and accepted the invitation. His labors being acceptable to the church and people, the society in a full meeting, all, with one solitary exception, voted to give him a call to become their pastor. After due consideration, the call was accepted, and in December following, the solemn relation was entered into by his ordination.

1827.—Will be long remembered on account of the great revival of religion which spread over the entire town, and continued for some months causing great accessions to the churches and a moral reformation generally.

In 1831, the church was again blessed with a revival which resulted in gathering a goodly number, including several heads of families, into the church.

Soon after this a church was formed in the villige of Collinsville, by means of which a very important portion of the Congregational church and society chose to remove their relation to that church and society, on account of the convenient location, and accordingly the relation heretofore existing was mutually and peacefully dissolved. But notwithstanding the great diminution of members, the first church, and society are, by the blessing of the Great Head of the Church, yet favored with the ordinances of the Gospel, and with the disposition and ability to support them to the present time.

Index

www.ingramcontent.com/pod-product-compliance
Lightning Source LLC
LaVergne TN
LVHW020627100826
845148LV00012B/2077

9781556139284